The Legal System of Scotland

Second edition

Derek Manson-Smith

April 2001

SCC Scottish
Consumer Council
Making all consumers matter

the
Stationery
Office

Applications for reproduction should be made in writing to HMSO, The Copyright Unit, St Clement's House, 2-16 Colegate, Norwich, NR3 1BQ.

The information contained in the publication is believed to be correct at time of manufacture. Whilst care has been taken to ensure that the information is accurate, the publisher can accept no responsibility for any errors or omissions or for changes to the details given.

A CIP catalogue record for this book is available from the British Library.

A Library of Congress CIP catalogue record has been applied for.

First published 2001

ISBN 0 11 4972893

Contents

Acknowledgements

I am grateful to Sarah O'Neill, Legal Officer at the Scottish Consumer Council, for her editorial guidance in revising this book and to the members of the Scottish Consumer Council's Legal Advisory Group, particularly Margaret Burns, for their comments on the draft.

I would also like to thank Fergus McNeil of the Criminal Justice Division in the Scottish Executive Justice Department, Catriona Whyte and Colin Lancaster of the Scottish Legal Aid Board, Philip Yelland of the Law Society of Scotland and Quintin Jardine of the Faculty of Advocates for their comments on particular chapters.

I have tried to provide an accurate reflection of the legal system of Scotland as it stood at 31 March 2001.

Derek Manson-Smith

April 2001

About the Scottish Consumer Council

The Scottish Consumer Council (SCC) was set up by government in 1975. Our purpose is to make all consumers matter. We do this by putting forward the consumer interest, particularly that of disadvantaged groups in society, by researching, campaigning and working with those who can make a difference to achieve beneficial change.

While producers of goods and services are usually well-organised and articulate when protecting their own interests, individual consumers very often are not. The people whose interests we represent are consumers of all kinds: they may be patients, tenants, parents, solicitors' clients, public transport users, or simply shoppers in a supermarket.

Consumers benefit from efficient and effective services in the public and private sectors. Service-providers benefit from discriminating consumers. A balanced partnership between the two is essential and the SCC seeks to develop this partnership by:

* carrying out research into consumer issues and concerns;

* informing key policy and decision-makers about consumer concerns and issues;

* influencing key policy and decision-making processes;

* informing and raising awareness among consumers.

Origins and sources of Scots law

1.1 Introduction

Following the Union of 1707, the laws and legal institutions of Scotland and of England and Wales were not merged but remained separate. Similarly, the laws and legal institutions of Ireland were not merged after the Union between Great Britain and Ireland of 1801. While the law of Northern Ireland is closely modelled on English law, which applies in England and Wales, Scots law is markedly different. It has its own originality, determined by its distinctive history and its relationship with other legal systems.

This was confirmed by the Scotland Act 1998, which in 1999 devolved certain powers from the United Kingdom Parliament to a Scottish Parliament. The Scottish Parliament can pass legislation on devolved matters without going through the United Kingdom Parliament in Westminster. The Acts of Union remain on the statute book and the Scotland Act ensures that the Acts of Union are construed in the light of the Scotland Act.

1.2 Types of legal systems

Legal systems are often distinguished from each other according to whether they are civilian law systems or common law systems.

Civilian law systems are those that are historically derived from Roman law. Most European countries adhere to civilian law systems.

Common law systems, however, are those derived from English law, and the countries which have common law systems are

England and Wales and Northern Ireland, most Commonwealth countries, and most of North America.

Historically, the essential difference between the two systems is that in civilian systems the rules of law are derived from first principles as expounded by the authoritative writings of jurists, while in common law systems the rules are derived from the decisions of judges in specific cases.

Scots law has its origins in the European civilian law systems, but has gradually developed similarities to the English common law approach, particularly the acceptance of judge-made law, or precedent, as a source of law.

1.3 Brief history of the development of Scots law

From the 11th century, Scotland was a feudal kingdom, which involved the granting of land in return for services, such as produce from the land or military service, and the courts were presided over by local landowners. While the monarch was in theory responsible for dispensing 'secular justice', that is, criminal and non-criminal or civil justice, the task was actually delegated to local 'sheriffs'. The church courts applied canon law in various matters including family matters and the inheritance of moveable property.

In the absence of universities in Scotland until the 15th century, and later of universities giving adequate training in law, Scots lawyers were educated in Europe, particularly in France, Germany, Flanders and the Netherlands, where Roman law was taught.

The structure of the judiciary began to take shape in 1532, when the Lords of Council and Session were permanently reorganised as a College of Justice with a wide civil (that is, non-criminal) jurisdiction. The 15 judges of 'the Session' became Senators of the College of Justice who sat together in one court.

In the 16th century the Faculty of Advocates and the Writers to the Signet evolved and were given the exclusive right to plead in court (as advocates) and to act as solicitors.

There continued to be three main differences between Scots and English law:

1) In the English common law courts between the 12th and the 19th centuries, court cases had to be started by using particular forms of action, so that each type of claim had its own name, and had to be raised in a particular way. Court action was not possible unless one of these forms of action was used, so there could not be a right without a legal remedy. In Scotland, the earlier forms of action, known as brieves and similar to the English writ, gave way to a more flexible procedural form (called a 'summons') which could be adapted to fit any number of different types of claim. As long as there was a right there were few procedural barriers to obtaining a remedy, as long as the action had been raised in the right court.

2) Scots law recognised the distinction between the strict letter of the law on the one hand, and the equitable discretion of judges to soften the rigours of the law on the other. But it did not follow the English practice of setting up equity (a right as founded on the laws of nature; moral justice) as a separate system, with its own rules and procedures and courts.

3) In England, juries were used in all civil cases to decide the facts. This was not so in Scotland.

In the late 17th century, Lord Stair, Lord President of the Court of Session, and the first of the so-called 'institutional writers', published his *Institutes of the Law of Scotland*. In this, Stair set out the whole of Scots law as a rational, comprehensive, coherent and practical set of rules deduced from common-sense principles. Where possible, Stair gleaned his law from reported Scottish decisions and statutes, or he was guided by Roman law, canon law or the Romano-Germanic systems.

Stair was followed in later centuries by other institutional writers such as Erskine, Bell and Hume, whose restatements of the law incorporated new law that had been developed by judges' decisions or enacted in statutes.

In 1707, the United Kingdom of Great Britain was created as a result of the Union of the Parliaments of Scotland and England.

Gradually, English law began to replace Roman law as the main external source of Scots law. Scots students were less likely to study law in Europe and the practice stopped with the Napoleonic wars. The House of Lords became the final court of appeal for Scots civil cases, and the English doctrine of judicial precedent, or subsequent cases being bound by decisions in earlier relevant cases, came to be more strictly applied.

The reform of the Court of Session in the early 19th century contributed to the move towards English legal methods. Two Inner House Divisions were created to hear appeals from Outer House judges and these appeal decisions were followed by Outer House judges in later cases. Despite the fact that judges in the House of Lords were likely to be English lawyers, judges in Scotland began to follow the decisions of the House of Lords. As Scotland's industrial, commercial and cultural experience began to grow more like that of England, it became obvious that English law was a more relevant source of law than Roman law. The influence of English law continued to grow, so that now, although a House of Lords decision on appeal from an English court is not binding on Scottish courts, it is nevertheless usually regarded as persuasive if the case concerns principles that apply in both legal systems. Scottish and English courts are not bound by each other's decisions but they do consider them persuasive, especially if they interpret United Kingdom statutes.

The civil (that is, non-criminal) law in Scotland rests on more generalised rights and duties than in England. Scots law still traditionally argues deductively from principles despite the influences of English law. Also, there continue to be many differences in the substantive law, that is the actual law concerned with rights and duties, to be contrasted with the legal process, that is court procedure. The present judicial system is substantially the same as it was following the Union of Parliaments in 1707. The Court of Session has almost universal civil jurisdiction, which means that almost any non-criminal case can be raised in the Court of Session as an alternative to the local sheriff court. The Court of Criminal Appeal, which hears appeals from decisions of the High Court of Justiciary as well as lower courts, was not set up until 1926. The local sheriff courts, presided over by full-time, legally-qualified judges, became the main local courts dealing with the bulk of the civil and criminal cases. The burgh courts or justices of the peace courts continued to deal with minor criminal offences. These were replaced by district courts in 1975, following reorganisation of local government, and continued to perform the same function after further local government reorganisation in 1996. Their future role was under review at the time of writing.

1.4 The Parliaments

1.4.1 Introduction

Before 1707, Scotland was an independent state with its own Parliament with an important law-making function. Although some Acts of the original Scottish Parliament remain in force, most have been repealed or can be regarded as no longer in force because of disuse.

1.4.2 The United Kingdom Parliament

In 1707, both English and Scottish Parliaments technically ceased to exist, and the United Kingdom Parliament with English, Scottish and Welsh members and peers, was constituted as a new legal institution, sitting in the same premises as the former English Parliament in Westminster.

Under the doctrine of sovereignty of Parliament, Acts of the United Kingdom Parliament were and continue to be absolutely binding on all courts, taking precedence over all other sources of law including the common law, except European Union law. Also, any Act of the United Kingdom Parliament can repeal or amend statutes whether passed by the United Kingdom Parliament, the former Scottish or English Parliaments or the current Scottish Parliament. The courts cannot challenge the United Kingdom Parliament's power of repeal or amendment, except to the extent that such an act is inconsistent with European Union law.

1.4.3 The Scottish Parliament

Pressure for constitutional change from the late 1960s led to a demand for a Scottish Parliament with law-making powers, which was approved by a referendum in 1997. Following the referendum, the United Kingdom Parliament passed the Scotland Act 1998, which devolved powers from the United Kingdom Parliament to Scotland, for which the Scottish Parliament was created in Edinburgh in May 1999.

The devolution settlement provided the Scottish Parliament in Edinburgh with devolved powers within the United Kingdom. The Scotland Act specifies the powers reserved to the United Kingdom Parliament. Those that are not reserved are devolved to the Scottish Parliament.

Devolved powers on matters such as education, health and local government, which used to be dealt with by the parliament in Westminster, are now decided by the Scottish Parliament. Reserved powers on matters with a United Kingdom or international aspect, such as social security, defence and foreign affairs, are reserved and decided by the United Kingdom Parliament.

The Scottish Parliament operates as a self-contained and fully-functioning parliament in its own right. Legislation on devolved matters can be passed by the Scottish Parliament without going through the United Kingdom Parliament, and it has powers to alter the rate of tax. While the United Kingdom Parliament retains the right to legislate on any matter, the convention of devolution is that the United Kingdom Parliament will not normally legislate on devolved matters without the consent of the Scottish Parliament.

The Scotland Act provides for the United Kingdom or Scottish Law Officers to challenge bills and Acts of the Scottish Parliament in the courts (see Chapter 11).

1.5 The European Union

1.5.1 Introduction

European Union derives from a set of international treaties concluded among a number of European countries since the 1950s. The principal treaties are the Treaty of Paris of 1951, which set up the European Coal and Steel Community, the Euratom Treaty of 1957, which created the European Atomic Energy Community, and the Treaty of Rome of 1957, which founded the European Economic Community. The Communities created by these treaties are legal persons distinct from their member states in international and domestic law, with their own independent rights, powers and duties. The treaties also provided for the creation of a parliamentary assembly, an inter-governmental council, an independent commission and a supervisory court.

The United Kingdom became a member of the European Communities on 1 January 1973, following the European Communities Act 1972 which gave effect to Community law in the United Kingdom and enabled the government to make regulations and orders implementing the country's obligations as a member of the Communities.

The European Communities evolved by way of other treaties, such as the Single European Act 1986, to form the European Community, and the Treaty on European Union 1992 (the Maastricht Treaty), which seeks a fuller European union by means of various institutional changes to the Community itself. In recognition of the importance of this development, the European Community became known as the European Union.

A further development was the Treaty of Amsterdam 1997, which concerns the Union's foreign policy and the free movement of its citizens. The latest phase of evolution is the Treaty of Nice 2000, which marks a new stage in the preparations for the enlargement of the European Union to include countries of central and eastern Europe, the Mediterranean and the Baltic. This treaty will amend the existing treaties and will enter into force once it has been ratified by the 15 member states in accordance with their respective constitutional procedures.

The European Union is a supra-national organisation, although it is not a federation like the United States of America. It makes laws through directives, regulations and decisions that have to be adopted by the national law of each member state (see 1.7). These apply to a large and increasing number of fields, ranging from consumer law to employment protection to intellectual property to immigration to company law.

1.5.2 The European Commission

The European Commission, which is based in Brussels, initiates and implements Union policy and legislates under its own powers and under those delegated by the Council of Ministers (see 1.5.3). The Commissioners, who are nominated by their governments, owe their allegiance to the Union, not to their governments. A civil service of directorates-general supports the Commissioners.

1.5.3 The Council of Ministers of the European Union

The Council of Ministers represents member states, coordinates their views and must approve most Union legislation. One minister from each member state's government sits on the Council, although at any one time different ministers may represent their government, depending on the subject in question.

As meetings of the Council are infrequent and the representative ministers are limited to the subject under discussion (for example, social issues, agricultural issues), the main work of the Council is carried out by the Committee of Permanent Representatives (known as COREPER, after the French abbreviation). COREPER is made up of national civil servants of the member states. It deals with all business that goes before the Council, and if its views are unanimous the Council accepts its decision.

1.5.4 The European Parliament

The European Parliament represents the electorate of member states and its members are directly elected. Formerly a largely supervisory, consultative and deliberative body, the parliament has acquired greater influence and power through a series of treaties, particularly the Treaty of Maastricht 1992 and the Treaty of Amsterdam 1997 (see 1.5.1). It is now a legislative parliament, exercising powers similar to those of national parliaments.

Membership of the European Parliament is allotted in different proportions to each member state. The parliament sits for one week a month in Strasbourg, where the European Parliament has it seat. Committees based in Brussels do most of its work, and it has a secretariat based in Luxembourg.

1.5.5 The European Court of Justice

The European Court of Justice, which sits in Luxembourg, ensures that Union law is correctly interpreted and observed by member states. Attached to it is the Court of First Instance, which was introduced to reduce the delays in cases coming before the Court of Justice. Some cases can be appealed from the Court of First Instance to the European Court of Justice.

The courts deal with several types of cases. They decide 'direct actions' where they hear the whole proceedings – these include actions against Union institutions. They also decide 'enforcement actions' brought by Union institutions against member states that are alleged to have failed to carry out their obligations under various treaties. Of more importance to the legal system of Scotland, the Court of Justice hears preliminary references from national courts and tribunals. Any national court or tribunal hearing a case that involves the interpretation or validity of Union law may, if it wishes, send that part of the case to the court for an authoritative ruling, which binds the national court. National courts have to apply European Union law – if there is any doubt, the issue can be referred to the Court of Justice. The national court decides questions of fact and gives the final decision (see 5.1).

1.6   The European Convention on Human Rights

The European Convention for the Protection of Human Rights and Fundamental Freedoms, usually known as the European Convention on Human Rights (ECHR), is a treaty signed by most western European counties, including the United Kingdom. The treaty was drawn up by the Council of Europe, a treaty organisation set up by European states to promote human rights.

The ECHR requires its signatories not to permit infringements of:

* A right to life

* Freedom from torture or inhuman or degrading treatment

* A right to liberty and security

* A right to family life

* A right to peaceful enjoyment of possessions

* A right to education

* A right to free elections

* A right to freedom of movement and residence

* The right of entry to a state of which one is a national and a right not to be expelled from it.

The European Commission on Human Rights is made up of a nominee of each signatory to the Convention. The Committee of Ministers of the Council of Europe is made up of the foreign ministers of countries that are members of the Council of Europe. The European Court of Human Rights has one judge from each signatory state.

1.6.1 The Human Rights Act 1998

While the European Convention on Human Rights has always been part of United Kingdom law, the Human Rights Act 1998 directly incorporates provisions from the convention into

United Kingdom law, so that the convention rights are enforceable in the United Kingdom courts. Formerly a case could be taken to the European Court of Human Rights only when domestic remedies had been exhausted.

The Human Rights Act makes it unlawful for a public authority to act incompatibly with convention rights, and allows for proceedings against the authority to be brought in an appropriate court or tribunal if it does so. Judicial review (see Chapter 11) provides a remedy in such circumstances.

The Act also requires all legislation to be interpreted and given effect as far as possible compatibly with convention rights. From its inception, the Scottish Parliament would be outwith its legislative competence if it passed a Scottish Bill that conflicted with the ECHR. Scottish judges can declare primary legislation incompatible with the convention. In such circumstances, a minister may amend the legislation to bring it into line with convention rights, or quash or disapply subordinate legislation (see Chapter 11).

The Scotland Act provides for dealing with the consequences of Acts of the Scottish Parliament or actions of the Scottish Executive that are found to be outwith their powers in relation to convention rights. The courts have powers to limit the retrospective effects of such Acts or actions. Provision is also made for the United Kingdom Parliament to make subordinate legislation to remedy the defect.

There are different procedures for dealing with Acts of the United Kingdom Parliament and actions of the United Kingdom government in these circumstances.

Scottish courts and tribunals must take account of the case law of the European Court of Human Rights, the European Commission on Human Rights and the Committee of Ministers of the Council of Europe. They are also bound to develop the common law compatibly with convention rights.

1.7   Sources of Scots law

The main sources of Scots law are judge-made law, certain legal writings having 'Institutional' authority (see 1.3) and, most importantly, legislation. The first two sources are sometimes referred to as the common law of Scotland. Legislation is formally-created law, comprising the law created by or under the authority of the United Kingdom and Scottish Parliaments, and by the European Union (see 1.5.1).

United Kingdom legislation consists of statutes (Acts of Parliament) made by the United Kingdom Parliament in Westminster on reserved matters and subordinate legislation authorised by the United Kingdom parliament.

Scottish legislation consists of Acts made by the Scottish Parliament on devolved matters (see 1.4.3), and subordinate legislation authorised by the parliament. Subordinate legislation in Scotland falls into two main groups:

* Regulations and rules made by Scottish Ministers or departments of the Scottish Executive. These are known as statutory instruments, which are published and are subject to a degree of parliamentary scrutiny and control, and they normally apply throughout Scotland. For example, the Education and Training (Scotland) Act 2000 provides for the payment of grants to assist individuals with the costs of lifelong learning; regulations under that Act, for instance, the Education and Training (Scotland) Regulations 2000 define 'arrangements' that qualify under the Act and provide for payment of grants to persons who are parties to such arrangements.

* Byelaws made by local authorities (which apply only in their areas) and other public authorities (which apply only within the sphere of their functions), under powers delegated to them by the Scottish Parliament. For example, the Glasgow City Council (Ledi Road) (Temporary Restriction) Order 2001 was made by Glasgow City Council under powers delegated by the Road Traffic Regulation Act 1984 to restrict certain motor vehicles on Ledi Road by reason of a weak bridge.

European Union legislation consists of primary legislation found in the treaties that established the framework and authority of the European Communities, and secondary legislation made by the codecision of the European Parliament, the Council of Ministers and the European Commission. Secondary legislation includes:

* Regulations, which have the force of law without the need for confirmation by the national legislatures of member states.

* Directives, which are binding as to the result to be achieved but have to implemented by member states in whatever way they feel appropriate.

* Decisions, which can be addressed to member states, corporations or individuals. They are binding but affect only those to whom they are addressed.

1.8   Further reading

Burrows, Noreen (ed.), *Greens Guide to European Law*. W Green, Edinburgh, 1995. £33.

Duncan, A G M, *Green's Glossary of Scottish Legal Terms*, 3rd edition. W Green, Edinburgh, 1992. £15.

Edward, David A O, *European Community Law: an introduction*, revised edition. Butterworths, Edinburgh, 1995. £22.

Finch, Valerie & Ashton, Christina, *Administrative Law in Scotland*. W Green, Edinburgh, 1997. £32.

Finch, Valerie & Ashton, Christina, *Scottish Human Rights Law*. W Green, Edinburgh, 2001. £32.

Gale, Sarah, *EC Law*. Butterworth, Edinburgh, 2000. £11.95

Meston, M C, *The Scottish Legal Tradition*. The Saltire Society, Edinburgh, 1991. £5.99.

Smith, S A de, *Constitutional and Administrative Law*, 8th edition. Penguin Books, London, 1998. £25.

2

Branches of Scots law

2.1 Introduction

The two most important branches of the law are civil and criminal law. Civil law is about deciding disputes between two parties – individuals or administrative authorities or commercial organisations. Criminal law is where the state prosecutes alleged criminal activity. Private prosecutions in the criminal courts are possible, although rare.

2.2 Civil law

The civil law can be separated into two parts – public law and private law.

2.2.1 Public law

Public law regulates and controls the exercise of political and administrative power within the state. It concerns the activities of the United Kingdom and Scottish Parliaments, the courts, Scottish Ministers (the collective term for members of the Scottish Executive, the devolved administration in Scotland), local government, and public bodies, for example, the regulators of privatised utilities, such as those for energy and telecommunications, and their relationships with private individuals.

In their relationships with private individuals, public bodies are within the competence of the Scottish Parliament except when they deal only with reserved matters (see 1.4.3) or have been designated as 'cross-border public authorities'. Cross-border public authorities are those that deal with matters both within and outwith the legislative competence of the Scottish

Parliament. They are within the competence of United Kingdom government ministers.

The Scotland Act 1998 provides for dealing with the consequences of Acts of the Scottish Parliament or actions of the Scottish Executive that are found to be outwith their powers (see 1.4.3 and 1.6.1).

Public law provides mechanisms to challenge the decisions made by such bodies, such as judicial review (see Chapter 11) and tribunals (see Chapter 6).

2.2.2 Private law

Private law deals with the rights and obligations of citizens among themselves. The major areas of private law are:

* Family law, which includes marriage, divorce, residence and guardianship of children, and adoption.

* The law of contract, which includes the sale of goods, consumer credit, insurance, and partnership.

* The law of delict, which deals mainly with civil wrongs for which the wrongdoer must pay compensation, such as defamation, damage to property or personal injury caused by negligence.

* The law of property, which concerns the right to enjoy property and the obligations arising from that enjoyment, ownership or possession of land or moveable property, the creation and administration of trusts, and succession (the division of someone's property following his or her death).

Other areas of private law include:

* Mercantile law, which deals with the law regulating trade, companies and bankruptcy.

* International private law, which regulates the jurisdiction of the Scottish courts in cases where people or property from outwith Scotland are involved. It determines whether Scots law or foreign law (in the sense of a legal system distinct from

Scots law, including English law and Northern Irish law) is applicable to a legal question and it provides for the recognition and enforcement in Scottish courts of foreign judgements.

2.3 Criminal law

The criminal law is not concerned with relationships between individuals or organisations, but rather with the maintenance of the peace and order of the community, and the prosecution and punishment of crime.

Generally, ignorance of the law is no defence. Therefore, in criminal matters, statute (that is Acts of the United Kingdom or Scottish Parliaments) or the common law should define crimes as clearly as possible, so that people have a fair notice of the restriction on their liberty of action.

In most cases, the prosecution has to prove that the person accused of the crime intended to do what he or she is accused of doing or failing to do.

More serious crimes are tried by a judge and jury on 'indictment'; others are tried by a judge without a jury (see 7.1).

Sometimes crimes are categorised by the kind of interest infringed — such as, offences against property (for example, theft), non-sexual injury (for example, assault), sexual offences (for example, rape), offences against the state (for example, treason), against public order and welfare (for example, breach of the peace), and against the course of justice (for example, perjury).

2.4 Further reading

Gordon, Alasdair, *Elements of Scots Law*. W Green, Edinburgh, 1997. £19.50.

Marshall, Enid A, *General Principles of Scots Law*, 7th edition. W Green, Edinburgh, 1999. £22.

3

The judicial system

The judicial system is made up of all the agencies that exist to resolve disputes, disagreements over claims and legal rights, and conflicts of interest, and to apply the law.

The main characteristic of the system is the existence of separate courts and tribunals for civil, criminal and administrative matters. Another characteristic is the division of the courts into inferior and superior courts. Inferior courts have jurisdiction locally, while superior courts have jurisdiction over the whole of Scotland. The sheriff court and the district court are known as inferior courts. The Court of Session, the High Court of Justiciary and the House of Lords are known as superior courts. A further characteristic is the division of courts and tribunals into those that have original jurisdiction, also known as courts or tribunals of first instance, which hear cases for the first time, and those of appellate jurisdiction, which hear appeals from other courts or tribunals. Some courts perform both functions at different times.

Litigation, or court action, in Scotland is generally an adversarial or contentious procedure, rather than an inquisitorial or investigative procedure, as is found in many other legal systems. This means that the judge usually does not act as an inquisitor and make an investigation but presides over a contest between two parties, ensuring that the rules of law are applied and followed, and decides the case on the basis of the legal arguments and the facts submitted.

In civil proceedings, it is for the person with a claim (the pursuer) to decide who to pursue (the defender), on what grounds of law, what facts to present, and who to call as witnesses. The defender can also present evidence and call witnesses. In criminal proceedings, it is for the Crown (the prosecutor) to decide who to prosecute (the accused), on what grounds of law, what evidence to produce, and who to call as witnesses. The accused person can similarly present evidence and call witnesses. The prosecutor may drop a charge at any stage and the judge cannot pass sentence on any finding of guilt unless asked to do so.

The two sides have to convince the jury, if there is one. The judge simply answers any questions on matters of fact or law, explains the law to the jury, and puts its verdict into effect.

4

The civil courts

4.1 The sheriff court

The sheriff court deals with the bulk of civil litigation in Scotland. It is a local court, presided over by the sheriff who is a legally-qualified judge and exercises a very wide jurisdiction (see 9.1.2). There is a sheriff court in every city and most towns.

Sheriff courts are organised into six sheriffdoms. These are: Grampian, Highland and Islands; Tayside, Central and Fife; Lothian and Borders; Glasgow and Strathkelvin; North Strathclyde; and South Strathclyde, Dumfries and Galloway. Each sheriffdom (except Glasgow and Strathkelvin) is divided into sheriff-court districts of which there are 49. For example, Tayside, Central and Fife is divided into the districts of Alloa, Arbroath, Cupar, Dundee, Dunfermline, Falkirk, Kirkcaldy and Stirling. There is provision for a total of 135 sheriffs, including 24 floating sheriffs, who are permanent, full-time sheriffs appointed to serve in any sheriffdom as required. Busier courts may have more than one sheriff, for example, Glasgow and Strathkelvin has twenty-two, with four floating sheriffs available if required, and Edinburgh has twelve, with two floating sheriffs.

Each sheriffdom has a sheriff principal who is responsible for the speedy and efficient conduct of business, a regional sheriff clerk, and a sheriff clerk for each court, who runs it from day-to-day.

The sheriff hears cases when they are first raised (at first instance) in the sheriff court of a district. In common law, the sheriff is 'judge ordinary of the bounds', that is, the judge with jurisdiction in all cases arising in his or her sheriffdom that are not allocated to other courts. The sheriff court also deals with appeals from, or review of, many local authority and other administrative decisions, for example, licensing appeals. Juries are not used in civil cases in the sheriff court. A case first heard by a sheriff can be appealed to the sheriff principal.

Many different types of action can be brought before the sheriff court. In civil cases, the pursuer must normally bring his or her case in the sheriffdom of the defender's domicile, that is, where he or she normally lives or has a place of business; or the place where a contract was to be carried out; or where the incident occurred that resulted in the legal action.

The sheriff court has exclusive jurisdiction in actions for sums of £1500 or less (this is expected to increase to £5000 in 2002) and in many statutory applications and appeals. The value of the subject matter that the court may deal with has, with very few exceptions, no upper limit, and a wide range of remedies may be granted. The sheriff court can consider actions for, among other things, debt, separation, divorce, damages, rent restriction, possession (for example, of a house), actions to make someone do something (for example, to deliver goods in fulfilment of a contract), actions affecting the use of property, leases and tenancies, and actions to regulate the residence of or contact with children. In practice, it deals mostly with debt and divorce.

The sheriff court cannot deal with certain types of cases. For example, judicial review (see Chapter 11), and under the Companies Act 1985, a sheriff cannot hear petitions, that is written applications to the court, to wind up a company with a paid-up share capital of greater than £120,000. Certain actions, for example, some of those involving status (declarator of marriage, nullity of marriage), are reserved for the Court of Session. Other cases, such as those concerning employment matters, are not normally heard in the sheriff court because they have their own tribunal (see 6.3).

4.2 The Court of Session

The Court of Session is the supreme civil court in Scotland. It is both a court of first instance and a court of appeal and sits only in Parliament House in Edinburgh. There is provision for 27 Court of Session judges. In addition, temporary judges may be appointed. One judge is seconded full-time as Chairman of the Scottish Law Commission (see 10.4). The Court of Session consists of two houses – the Outer House and the Inner House.

4.2.1 The Outer House

The 19 more junior judges, called Lords Ordinary, form the Outer House. They are exclusively concerned with deciding cases for the first time, and sit alone, usually without a jury.

The Outer House's jurisdiction is wide and includes all kinds of civil claims unless the law expressly excludes them. It covers actions on commercial cases, contract, reparation, property and personal status, petitions for the appointment of judicial factors and curators, that is, people appointed by a court to act for someone who is unable to act alone, on matters of succession and trusts, and for the winding up of a company. However, most cases concern debt, divorce and personal injury.

Juries can be used in certain types of Court of Session cases, such as personal injury claims or defamation.

4.2.2 The Inner House

The Inner House is made up of two Divisions, each with four judges. The Lord President of the Court of Session presides over the First Division and the Lord Justice-Clerk presides over the Second Division. An Extra Division of three judges sits frequently to relieve the pressure of business on the court.

Mostly, each Division acts as an appeal court to review decisions of the Outer House judges and of other inferior courts. In practice, each Division normally sits with three judges. Decisions are by a majority, with each judge having one vote. Sometimes, if a case is particularly important or difficult and the court wishes to review a previous decision to resolve the difficulty, a Division can summon additional judges to make up a larger court of five or more judges.

4.3 The House of Lords

The 'House of Lords' is actually the Appellate Committee of the House of Lords, which is made up of Lords of Appeal chosen from the Lord Chancellor, the Lords of Appeal in Ordinary and other peers who have held high judicial office. Informally, they are referred to as the Law Lords; lay peers do not take part in judicial proceedings.

The House of Lords hears cases at first instance, that is when they are first raised, only in breach of privilege, disputed claims to a peerage and impeachment. It is effectively the final court of appeal from the civil courts, although subject to decisions of the European Court of Justice on European Union law matters.

Normally, five Lords of Appeal sit to hear an appeal; the quorum is three. Usually at least two are Scottish. However, there is no requirement that a Scottish Law Lord must be present to hear a Scottish appeal and in consequence, non-Scottish judges with little or no knowledge of Scots law can decide Scottish appeals.

4.4 The European Court of Justice

The European Court of Justice (see 1.5.5) exists to ensure compliance with the law in the application and interpretation of the treaties and is the European Union's supreme court. The judges owe their allegiance to the court and not to their home countries.

The Court of First Instance was created in 1989 to strengthen the judicial safeguards available to individuals by introducing a second tier of judicial authority and enabling the Court of Justice to concentrate on its essential task, the uniform interpretation of Community law.

The Court of Justice has one judge from each member state and two judges from one of the larger states. The court may sit either as a whole or with fewer numbers, depending on the type and importance of the case. The Court of First Instance has one judge from each member state. Each court has advocates-general who present preliminary reasoned judgements to the courts.

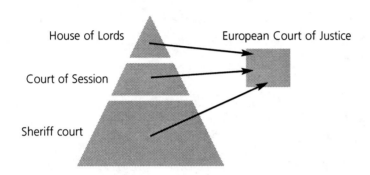

Figure 1. The civil courts (simplified)

4.5 Courts of special jurisdiction

Courts of special jurisdiction have jurisdiction in particular kinds of claim only.

* The Scottish Land Court deals with agricultural tenancies, crofting tenancies and rent review arbitrations.

* The Restrictive Practices Court, which is a United Kingdom court, deals with restrictive and unfair trade practices and claims for the exemption of goods from the rule abolishing resale price maintenance.

* The Lands Valuation Appeal Court hears appeals from the decisions of the local valuation appeal committees on the rateable values of commercial property.

* The Employment Appeal Tribunal, which by its constituent Act is declared to be a court, has jurisdiction throughout the United Kingdom and hears appeals from employment tribunals.

* The Court of Exchequer in Scotland deals with tax disputes.

* The Registration of Voters Appeal Court deals with appeals from the sheriff concerning the registration of parliamentary electors.

* The Election Petition Court hears petitions to set aside the election of Members of Parliament on the grounds of corruption, illegality and the like.

* The Court of the Lord Lyon King of Arms has jurisdiction in disputes over the right to bear coats-of-arms. Prosecutions may be brought to the Lord Lyon Court against the wrongful assumption or use of arms.

* The Court of Teinds deals with tithes or tenth parts of harvests once paid by the laity to maintain the church. Teind law is now unimportant and the court's business is almost wholly formal.

4.6 Administrative functions of courts

Both the Court of Session and the sheriff court have certain administrative functions. For example, the Court of Session supervises company liquidations, bankruptcies and the management by judicial factors of the estates of children, or of people who are incapable of managing their affairs, such as someone with a mental disorder. The sheriff court deals with petitions for the adoption of children and bankruptcy proceedings, and deals with confirming some of the arrangements for distributing the estate of someone who has died.

4.7 Further reading

An Introduction to the Scottish Court Service. Available free of charge from the Scottish Court Service, Hayweight House, 23 Lauriston Street, Edinburgh EH3 9DQ.

See also: http://www.scotcourts.gov.uk

5

Civil judicial procedure

5.1 Introduction

A civil dispute arises when two or more parties disagree on matters of fact or law or both that affect their legal rights and duties. Most civil disputes are settled by agreement or compromise. When a dispute cannot be settled in this way, it can often only be resolved by taking it before a court or tribunal. However, some disputes may be resolved by more informal methods such as mediation, arbitration or other forms of alternative dispute resolution (see 5.8).

Civil procedure (like criminal procedure) is usually adversarial. In other words, it is a legal contest between the two parties, and the judge, or in some cases the jury, decides a case on the basis of the facts alleged and proved by the parties or their lawyers and their legal arguments. The person who starts the case (the pursuer) has to prove it 'on the balance of probabilities' and puts before the court evidence and arguments that support his or her case and entitle him or her to a remedy. The person called to answer the case (the defender) may claim that the pursuer has not proved the case, or submit evidence and arguments to show why the pursuer should not receive what he or she is claiming. If the defender does not appear to defend the case, a 'decree in absence', that is a judicial decision made in someone's absence, may be issued against him or her. The parties can settle a dispute at any stage before a case is decided, either in court or out of court.

In any case that involves the interpretation or validity of European Union law, national courts may, and in some cases they must, suspend the case until the matter has been referred to the European Court of Justice for a ruling. Once the European

Court has made a ruling, the case then comes back to the national court, which applies the ruling to the particular facts of the case and decides accordingly. Where the matter comes up in a House of Lords case, which is the ultimate national court of appeal in civil cases, the House of Lords has no option but to refer it to the European Court.

5.2 The Court of Session

The Court of Session has jurisdiction over all civil claims brought in Scotland except in cases where the law places jurisdiction solely with the sheriff court, a court of special jurisdiction (see 4.5) or a statutory tribunal.

Cases brought to the Court of Session are almost always brought as 'actions' or 'petitions'. The object of an action is to enforce a legal right against a defender who resists it or to protect a legal right that the defender is infringing. The object of a petition is generally to obtain from the Court power to do something or to require something to be done but which the petitioner has no legal right to do, apart from judicial authority.

5.2.1 Actions in the Court of Session

An action in the Court of Session is begun when one party, the pursuer, serves (usually by post) on the other party, the defender, a summons which has been registered and signeted in the offices of the court. The signet is a seal by which certain writs in the name of the Sovereign, including a Court of Session summons, are verified.

The summons or initial writ, that is the legal document that commences the court proceedings against someone, states that the defender should attend court, otherwise a decree in absence may be granted against him or her. Attached to it are: a request to grant the remedy the pursuer wants (for example, payment of a sum of money in reparation for a personal injury caused by the defender); a brief statement of the facts as the pursuer sees them, which, if proved, should be enough to entitle the pursuer to the remedy he or she seeks, and the legal basis for the pursuer's claim.

The defender has a chance to put forward his or her statement of the facts, either accepting or rejecting the pursuer's statement, together with legal arguments in support of his or her own case. Both parties then have an opportunity to adjust their own case in response to the statements, allegations and arguments put forward by the other side. The matter then goes forward for decision by the court.

If the dispute concerns questions of law, there will be a debate in court between lawyers on those legal questions and, if the parties agree about the facts, the court will give its decision granting, or refusing, the remedy sought by the pursuer.

Where there is a dispute about the facts, evidence will be submitted to the judge sitting without a jury or in rare cases, before the judge sitting with a jury. In civil cases, the jury is twelve.

5.2.2 Petitions in the Court of Session

A petition is an application by one side only to the court. Petitions are often used where the petitioner and the respondent to the petition are not in dispute but where the law nevertheless requires the court's approval for some matter. Examples include petitions for the sequestration of an insolvent person, for the liquidation of a company, for an order enabling a person to adopt a child, for the appointment of a judicial factor to administer property, or for the alteration of the purposes of a trust.

Some types of petition, however, are often contentious, such as petitions to regulate the residence of children. A petition is presented to the court, and the court then decides who should receive service or intimation of the petition. Any respondent of the petition may lodge answers in much the same way as any defender to a summons can lodge defences.

The Court of Session also has an inherent equitable power, known the *nobile officium* (its noble office), to provide a remedy where none is available under existing legislation or the rules of common law. Someone wishing to ask the Court of Session to use this power must do so by submitting a petition.

5.3 Sheriff court civil procedure

The procedure followed in the sheriff court depends on the value of the claim. There are three different systems: small claims for claims of £750 or less, summary cause for claims over £750 and less than £1500, and ordinary cause for claims over £1500. In 2002, these limits are expected to be increased (see 5.3.1, 5.3.2 and 5.3.3).

5.3.1 Small claims procedure

The small claims procedure, which deals with claims of £750 or less, was introduced in 1988. In 2002, the limit is expected to be increased to £1500.

Although technically part of summary cause procedure, small claims has its own rules and is meant to be faster, simpler, cheaper and more informal. The procedure may be initiated or defended by an ordinary citizen, for example, to recover a consumer debt. However, the majority tend to be raised by large businesses, local authorities, public utilities and mail-order companies.

The procedure is initiated by the pursuer filling in a pre-printed form (the summons) and returning it to court. If the pursuer is an ordinary individual, not a company, the sheriff clerk will send the summons to the person against whom the claim is made. Although the procedure is intended to be informal, this does not always happen, as complicated questions of law can arise and be dealt with in an adversarial fashion.

5.3.2 Summary cause procedure

Claims valued at between £750 and £1500 are dealt with under summary cause procedure. In 2002, it is expected that the lower limit will be increased to £1500 and the upper limit to £5000.

Summary cause procedure is generally more complicated than small claims procedure. However, many actions are straightforward and the sheriff has large discretion over procedure. Most claims are for recovery of a debt or repossession of property.

5.3.3 Ordinary cause procedure

Claims valued at over £1500 are dealt with under ordinary cause procedure. In 2002, the limit is expected to be increased to £5000.

The procedure in ordinary cause actions is similar to that in actions in the Court of Session (see 5.2.1), but there are time limits which apply in the sheriff court that do not apply in the Court of Session. After a period of adjustment of the written statements, the action then goes to an 'options hearing', where the sheriff decides what the issues in dispute between the parties really are, and what further procedure is needed, bearing in mind the need to progress the case at a reasonable speed.

Most cases relating to family matters, for example, those relating to the end of a marriage, or the residence of children, will need the parties involved in the action to attend the options hearing. This is to see if the parties can agree anything. The sheriff can refer family cases to an appropriate family mediation service (see 5.8.2).

In civil proceedings, jury trial has been abolished in the sheriff court.

5.3.4 Summary and other special applications

The object of a summary application, which is regulated by specific rules of court, is to obtain from the sheriff power to do something or require something to be done for which the sheriff's authority is needed. This is usually regulated by statute but in some cases by the common law.

The sheriff court disposes of a wide variety of administrative and miscellaneous matters by this procedure. The procedure in a summary application is at the sheriff's discretion. In other special applications, the procedure is wholly or partly prescribed by statute or act of sederunt (procedural rules made by judges of the Court of Session).

5.3.5 Going to court

An individual who goes to court may always represent him or herself, or be represented by a solicitor, solicitor-advocate or an advocate. It is much easier for a person to act on his or her own or with the help of a representative who is not legally qualified in small claims and summary cause actions than in ordinary cause or Court of Session actions.

Small claims, summary cause actions (first calling only) and proceedings under the Debtors (Scotland) Act 1987 are the only circumstances when representation by non-lawyers is permitted.

5.4   Special courts and tribunals

Special courts and tribunals have a wide range of procedures, depending on the purposes for which they were established. Some special courts and tribunals have formal rules of procedure, while many tribunals are informal (see Chapter 6).

5.5 *Remedies*

The more common civil remedies are:

* Specific implement – an order to do something, for example, to deliver goods or perform a service.

* Interdict – an order prohibiting the commission or continued commission of a legal wrong, for example, against broadcasting an allegedly defamatory statement.

* Declarator – a pronouncement that a particular individual or corporate body has a specific right or duty, for example, that a local authority has a duty to house a homeless person.

* Damages – an order to pay financial compensation for loss or injury caused by fault or neglect, for example, an award of damages for loss caused by breach of contract or personal injuries resulting from fault or neglect.

* Reduction – an order that sets aside as invalid a document that is prejudicial to the pursuer's rights, for example, a will.

* Aliment – an order to provide financial support for a spouse, for example, in a divorce action.

* Consistorial remedies – judicial separation of two spouses or divorce.

* Protection – securing the possession of property.

In addition, there are numerous specific remedies provided by statute for specific circumstances. The Court of Session also has the power of judicial review over the decisions of lower courts and tribunals and of government, on the grounds of procedural impropriety, such as the lack of natural justice (for instance, not hearing both sides of a case) or *ultra vires* (acting beyond one's powers) (see Chapter 11), and its *nobile officium* (see 5.2.2).

5.6　Diligence

If a court's order is not obeyed, the pursuer can enforce it through 'diligence'. The essential first step in diligence is a charge – a formal demand for payment – which is served by a messenger-at-arms (for a Court of Session decree) or sheriff-officer (for a sheriff-court decree). The common forms of diligence are:

* Arrestment – arresting a debtor's funds held by a third party, such as a bank.

* Earnings arrestment – arresting a debtor's earnings. There are legal limits to the amount of earnings that can be arrested.

* Poinding (pronounced 'pinding') – moveable property owned by and in the possession of the debtor is identified and valued. The property cannot be disposed of, and if the debt is not paid, the pursuer can request permission from the court to remove and sell the property by auction. Certain goods are exempt from poinding, for example, essential furniture. Note that under the Abolition of Poindings and Warrant Sales Act 2001, poindings and warrant sales will cease on or before 31 December 2002, and are likely to be replaced by an alternative form of diligence.

* Inhibition – forbidding the sale of heritable property, that is, land and buildings.

In Scotland, imprisonment for non-payment of debt can only occur for non-payment of aliment.

5.7 Appeals

Most decisions taken by a court or tribunal can be appealed. Appeals may be on a point of fact or law or both. An appeal court can agree with the decision of the lower court, substitute its own judgement, or send the case back to the lower court for further procedure or a final decision, taking the judgement of the appeal court into account.

In civil cases, appeals depend on the court and the procedure used:

- A decision of a judge in the Outer House of the Court of Session can be appealed to the Inner House on a point of law or fact or on the way the judge exercised discretion, and may be further appealed to the House of Lords.

- In small claims, appeal is to the sheriff principal on a point of law only.

- In summary cause actions, appeal is to the sheriff principal on a point of law only, and then to the Inner House of the Court of Session, and finally to the House of Lords.

- In ordinary cause actions, appeal is to the sheriff principal, and then to the Court of Session. On a point of law only, appeal can then be made to the House of Lords.

- Appeal from the decisions of special courts and tribunals depends on the particular court or tribunal involved.

5.8 Alternative Dispute Resolution

Alternative dispute resolution (ADR) provides alternative ways of resolving disputes, usually outwith the courts. ADR may be used in family, commercial, consumer and community disputes. The most common forms of ADR include arbitration and mediation.

5.8.1 Arbitration

The procedure in arbitration is agreed by the parties to it, with the degree of formality influenced by the balance of fact or law involved. Lawyers may be involved, there may be legal arguments, inspections may be made of the subject matter or premises in dispute, or experts may be consulted, depending on the particular arbitration.

In going to arbitration, the parties agree to exclude the jurisdiction of the courts. While a court may state an opinion on a point of law referred to it during arbitration, there is no appeal from the arbiter's decision. However, a court may reduce an award where, for example, it decides there has been a conflict of interest, or the arbiter has dealt with a point outwith the terms of reference, or there has been a denial of natural justice.

5.8.2 Mediation

Mediation is a process of structured negotiations where the disputing parties are assisted by a neutral third party to reach their own resolution to their conflict. Mediation is most often used in family, neighbourhood and commercial disputes. It is sometimes used during a court action. For example, the Children (Scotland) Act 1995 allows a court to refer a couple to mediation at any time during a family action where there are children.

ADR activities may be funded in a number of ways. For example, within the commercial sphere, it is normal practice for the disputing parties to share equally the costs of mediation. Legal aid is available for eligible partners who wish to use mediation to resolve issues arising from divorce or separation (see 12.3). Legal aid is also likely to be made available for mediation in non-family civil disputes.

5.9 Fatal accident and sudden death inquiries

Following a fatal accident at work, death in legal custody (for example, in prison or a police station), and other cases of sudden, suspicious or unexplained death, a public inquiry may be arranged by the procurator fiscal. There are no coroners in Scotland.

Information is collected by the procurator fiscal and presented to a sheriff or sheriff principal. Interested parties may appear personally and take part in the inquiry or may be represented by a solicitor or advocate. Interested parties could include relatives of the person who has died, employers, fellow employees, trade union representatives, and inspectors of factories and mines.

The inquiry is held in public and conducted on the lines of a civil trial. At the end, the sheriff makes a decision in which he or she sets out the circumstances affecting the death, including any precautions that may have avoided it and any defects that may have contributed to it. Decisions do not usually include findings of fault against anyone and may include recommendations for safer practices.

The decision cannot be used in any subsequent civil or criminal proceedings arising from the accident and witnesses are not required to answer any question that may incriminate them.

5.10   Further reading

Note that the small claims and summary cause rules are expected to change in 2002.

Ervine, W Cowan H, *Small Claims Handbook*, 2nd edition. W Green, Edinburgh (in progress).

McCulloch, William & Laing, Evelyn, *Ordinary Cause Rules*. Clt Professional Publishing, 1998. £32.

Mays, Richard, *Summary Cause Procedure in the Sheriff Court*. Butterworth, Edinburgh, 1996. £37.

6

Tribunals

6.1 Introduction

Tribunals exercise judicial or quasi-judicial functions in that they exist to resolve disputes about the law or the technical application of the law, but they are not technically courts of law. The number of tribunals has grown considerably in recent years. They are perceived as having advantages over courts in being able to deal with cases more informally, more cheaply, more quickly, and with specific expertise.

There is a wide range of different kinds of tribunals, varying in the kind of dispute that they deal with, how they are administered, their memberships and the formality of their procedures.

Tribunals deal with disputes between individuals and public authorities, for example, social security appeal tribunals that hear appeals against Benefits Agency decisions on eligibility for some social security benefits. But some tribunals deal with disputes between private individuals or organisations, for example, employment tribunals, the Lands Tribunal for Scotland.

Some tribunals are organised on a national basis. For example, the Office of Social Security and Child Support Commissioners deals with applications for leave to appeal and appeals from social security, medical, disability and child support appeal tribunals on a United Kingdom basis. Some are administered by local authorities, for example, education appeal committees, and valuation appeal committees which hear council tax appeals.

The composition of tribunals varies. Often there is a legally-qualified chairman with two other members who have specific expertise, although some social security tribunals operate with a legally-qualified chairman alone. Other tribunals, such as the medical services committees, which hear complaints against general practitioners, may have up to seven members. Some tribunals are composed entirely of lay people.

Sometimes a dispute may be appealed through a hierarchy of tribunals. For example, certain questions of income tax from the Inspector of Taxes to the Special or General Commissioners of Income Tax, or a decision of an immigration officer to an adjudicator to the Immigration Appeal Tribunal. Appeals on a point of law may be taken to the Court of Session from most tribunals. Where there is no specific right of appeal, a decision of a tribunal may be brought before the Court of Session by the procedure of judicial review (see Chapter 11), but only on the grounds of refusal to exercise jurisdiction, acting in excess of jurisdiction, procedural irregularity or breach of natural justice.

The Council on Tribunals, which has a Scottish Committee based in Edinburgh, supervises most tribunals. Certain tribunals that deal with disciplinary matters in particular professions (such as the Scottish Solicitors Discipline Tribunal (see 14.2.4) and the General Medical Council) are not subject to supervision by the Council on Tribunals.

Two examples of particular tribunals are given below.

6.2 Children's hearings

In Scotland, children under the age of 16 who may be in need of care and protection or who have committed an offence can be brought to a children's hearing. Children under 16 are only considered for prosecution in the courts where serious offences, such as murder, rape or assault to the danger of life are involved.

The children's hearing system is unique to Scotland and represents one of the radical changes initiated by the Social Work (Scotland) Act 1968 and continued by the Children (Scotland) Act 1995. The principles underlying the system were recommended by the Committee on Children and Young Persons (The Kilbrandon Committee), which found that children appearing before the courts, whether they had committed offences or were in need of care and protection, had common needs for social and personal care.

6.2.1 The children's panel

A children's hearing is a statutory lay tribunal composed of three members of the children's panel for the local authority area. Members are volunteers who are non-lawyers and who come from a wide range of occupations, neighbourhoods and income groups in the local community. Scottish Ministers, on the advice of the local Children's Panel Advisory Committee, appoint them to the panel.

6.2.2 The reporter

A child who may be in need of compulsory measures of care must be referred to the reporter to the children's panel, who is an independent official. Sources of referral may be the police, social work and education authorities, or indeed any member of the public. The reporter has a duty to make an initial investigation before deciding what, if any, action is necessary in the child's interests.

6.2.3 Grounds of referral

A child may be brought before a hearing on a number of grounds. These include being beyond the control of any relevant person; falling into bad associations or being exposed to moral danger; suffering through lack of parental care; being a victim of physical injury or sexual abuse; failing to attend school; having committed an offence. A child may also be referred when certain offences against children to which special provisions apply have been committed against him or her, or because he or she is likely to become a member of the same household as such a child, or a member of the same household as a person who committed one of those offences.

In certain circumstances, a child may be detained on a warrant in a place of safety for not more than 22 days, pending a decision by a children's hearing.

6.2.4 The hearing

The hearing is informal and in private. It is the purpose of the children's hearing to decide whether the child is in need of compulsory measures of care and, if so, what these measures should be. In doing so it must consider any social, education or other background reports, consider whether it is necessary to appoint a safeguarder to safeguard the interests of the child in the proceedings, and discuss the situation fully with the child, his or her parents, and any representatives, if present.

The hearing cannot make a disposal or discuss the case unless the child and his or her parents accept the reasons why the child has been referred. If these 'grounds' are not accepted, then the case will be sent to be proved at the sheriff court.

6.2.5 Disposals

If the hearing decides that compulsory measure of care are appropriate, it will impose a supervision requirement that can be renewed until the child is 18. The requirement may be that the child lives at home under the supervision of the social work department, or that the child should live away from home with relatives, foster parents or in a residential home. A hearing cannot fine the child or the parents.

6.2.6 Appeals

Rights of appeal are on a point of law only to a sheriff and from there to the Court of Session. It is also possible to appeal to the Court of Session if the proper procedures have not been followed.

6.3 Employment tribunals

Employment tribunals have jurisdiction over a wide range of issues connected with employment including, for example, claims for equal pay, complaints about sex, racial or disability discrimination, failure to pay maternity pay, failure to provide full pay, unfair dismissal, unreasonable exclusion from a trade union. An employment tribunal has three members – a legally-qualified chairman and two lay members, one representing employers and the other employees (although in some circumstances the chairman may sit and hear cases on his or her own).

Appeal on a question of law may be made to the Employment Appeal Tribunal. The tribunal (see 4.5) is made up of judges of the English High Court, one or more judges of the Court of Session, and lay members with specialist knowledge of industrial relations.

6.4 The Criminal Injuries Compensation Authority

The Criminal Injuries Compensation Authority was set up under the Criminal Injuries Compensation Act 1995 to administer the tariff-based Criminal Injuries Compensation Scheme that came into effect for all applications from 1 April 1996. The scheme was formerly administered by the Criminal Injuries Compensation Board, which ceased to exist after 31 March 2000, when all applications under consideration were transferred to the Criminal Injuries Compensation Authority.

The scheme deals with claims for compensation, in certain circumstances, from victims of crimes of violence and from people hurt as a result of attempts to arrest offenders or prevent offences. A victim includes a dependant of someone who dies as a result of a criminal injury.

Standard awards are made according to a tariff, which sets out fixed levels of compensation and the level and corresponding amount of compensation for each description of injury.

Decisions taken by the authority may be appealed to the Criminal Injuries Compensation Appeals Panel, whose members are legally qualified and are appointed by the Home Secretary and Scottish Ministers.

6.5 Further reading

Norrie, Kenneth, *Children's Hearings in Scotland.* W Green, Edinburgh, 1997. £42.50.

Children's Hearing System: http://www.childrens-hearings.co.uk

7

The criminal courts

7.1 Introduction

In Scotland, crimes are prosecuted in the district court, the sheriff court, and the High Court of Justiciary. The Crown prosecutes all cases, except where public authorities have statutory powers to prosecute for specific offences and on the rare occurrence of a private prosecution (see 8.3). Generally, the district court deals with minor offences, and the sheriff court deals with more serious offences. The most serious offences, such as rape and murder, are dealt with in the High Court.

The more serious crimes are tried 'on indictment', where a judge sits with a jury. Less serious offences are tried before a sheriff or before one or three justices of the peace (in a district court). Most criminal prosecutions in Scotland take place in the sheriff courts.

7.2 The district court

There are district courts in each local authority area. They handle prosecutions of breaches of the peace and certain minor offences committed within the district. The courts are presided over by lay justices of the peace. In Glasgow, there are also legally-qualified stipendiary (that is, salaried) magistrates who sit in the district court.

The jurisdiction of the court includes all statutory offences that are capable of being tried summarily, although in the case of road traffic offences the court cannot deal with cases where disqualification from driving is an option. The court has no jurisdiction over children under 16 years of age.

The powers of punishment of a district court are limited to up to 60 days' imprisonment or a fine of £2500 or both, although a stipendiary magistrate has the same sentencing power as a sheriff has under summary procedure.

At the time of writing, a review of the district courts was examining whether there should be a re-balancing of the work between the sheriff and district courts. It was also examining whether lay justice should be replaced by professional arrangements, for example, increased use of stipendiary magistrates, and whether district courts should continue to operate under local authority control.

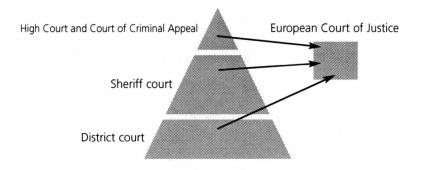

High Court and Court of Criminal Appeal   European Court of Justice

Sheriff court

District court

Figure 2. The criminal courts (simplified)

7.3   The sheriff court

The sheriff court deals with more serious cases than the district court. It can deal with any offences committed within the sheriffdom that are not reserved for the High Court (rape, murder, attempted murder, etc.), including those that may be dealt with by the district court.

In less serious cases tried under summary procedure, a sheriff's powers of punishment are limited to three months' imprisonment, unless there are previous convictions, or a fine of up to £5000, although these powers may be limited or widened for offences by statute.

Solemn procedure is used in more serious cases where the indictment attracts a sentence on conviction in excess of three months' imprisonment or a fine of more than £5000. Trials under solemn procedure are heard before a sheriff sitting with a jury. If a sheriff feels that in any particular case his or her powers are too limited, the convicted person can be sent to the High Court for sentence.

7.4 The High Court of Justiciary

The High Court is Scotland's supreme criminal court. There is no appeal from it to the House of Lords. It was established in 1672, replacing the Court of the Justiciar. The judges are the same as those in the Court of Session but wear different robes.

The person appointed as Lord President of the Court of Session is also head of the High Court, but there he is known as the Lord Justice-General. The second most senior judge is known as the Lord Justice-Clerk. The High Court is both a trial court and a court of appeal.

As a trial court, the High Court sits in Edinburgh but also travels to different parts of Scotland – to places where there are courts large enough to accommodate it, including Glasgow, Stirling, Oban, Inverness, Aberdeen, Dundee, Perth, Dumfries, Jedburgh and Ayr, or at any convenient town or near where the crime being tried was carried out.

The High Court has jurisdiction over all of Scotland, and covers all types of crime not specifically reserved to another court. Only the High Court can deal with allegations of treason, murder, rape, incest, certain offences under the Official Secrets Act, obstruction of officers of the court (called 'deforcement of messengers'), and breach of duty by magistrates.

Normally, only one judge sits at a trial but exceptionally, in cases of importance or difficulty, two or more, usually three, may sit. There is always a jury. The prosecution is conducted by a law officer or advocate depute (see 8.3) and the accused person is defended by an advocate or a solicitor-advocate.

As an appeal court, the High Court sits only in Edinburgh, where appeals are heard by three or more judges. All appeals from the district court, the sheriff court and the High Court come before this court, and it hears appeals in cases referred to it by Scottish Ministers. It also has power to deal with unusual or unforeseen circumstances in the exercise of its equitable power, known as the *nobile officium* (see 8.8).

7.5 Further reading

An Introduction to the Scottish Court Service. Available free from Scottish Court Service, Hayweight House, 23 Lauriston Street, Edinburgh EH3 9DQ.

See also: http://www.scotcourts.gov.uk

8

Criminal justice

8.1 Introduction

Following the Union of 1707, Scottish criminal justice continued to be very different from that in England and Wales. The Scotland Act 1998 provided protection for the system following devolution in 1999 by entrenching the Lord Advocate as head of the systems of criminal prosecutions and the investigation of deaths.

8.2 Criminal investigation and apprehension

The procurator fiscal has responsibility at local level for the investigation and prosecution of crime. In practice, the police or a statutory reporting agency, such as HM Customs and Excise, carry out the initial investigation. They may question a suspect, demand his or her name and address and ask for an explanation of the circumstances that have aroused suspicion. They may also question witnesses. An individual suspected of a crime that is punishable by imprisonment may be detained at police or other premises without being arrested, but for no more than six hours without being charged. During this period, a suspect may be searched, fingerprinted and questioned but need not answer any questions except to provide his or her name and address. The suspect may require that a solicitor and one other person are told of his or her detention, but this may be delayed where necessary to prevent or detect crime. The police may also search anyone suspected of carrying an offensive weapon in public and detain him or her for that purpose.

If a person is arrested, he or she must be charged with a crime and cautioned that he or she need say nothing but that anything he or she does say may be taken down and used in evidence.

Failure to caution a suspect or unreasonable harshness in questioning by the police may result in any alleged confession being held to be inadmissible at a subsequent trial. The case is then referred to the procurator fiscal. Like a detainee, a person in custody may require that a solicitor and one other person be told of the arrest, normally without delay.

The police must take all precautions against the unreasonable and unnecessary detention of an accused person. In most cases, someone who has been charged is then released, but the police may require a written undertaking to appear at a particular court at a specified time. A report that the accused has been charged with a particular offence and a summary of the evidence is then sent to the procurator fiscal. In due course, if the procurator fiscal decides to go ahead with a prosecution, the accused person has to appear in court to answer the charges.

Someone who has been in custody will normally appear at the local sheriff or district court on the next working day. Someone in custody has a right to see a solicitor before appearing in court. 'Duty solicitors', provided through the legal aid system, can represent people in custody at their first appearance (see 12.4.1).

If the procurator fiscal is satisfied that there is sufficient evidence in a case, he or she will consider what action is required in the public interest. This will include no action, the use of an alternative to prosecution or prosecution. He or she has a statutory duty, in terms of the Scotland Act 1998, to act in a way that is compatible with the convention rights as defined in the Human Rights Act 1998. The procurator fiscal's discretion to prosecute or not is a principal feature of the system. There is no rule of law in Scotland that a criminal offence must be prosecuted.

8.2.1 *Alternatives to prosecution*

There are a number of alternatives to prosecution.

* The procurator fiscal may warn someone who has been reported by the police that his or her behaviour is unacceptable and that any repetition will result in prosecution.

* The offender may be offered the option of accepting guidance from a voluntary organisation, such as Alcoholics Anonymous, or the supervision of a social worker.

* In certain minor cases, where there is an identifiable victim, a background of conflict between the two parties, or an indication that the accused is in a position to make amends, the procurator fiscal may arrange supervised reparation or mediation between the alleged offender and victim.

* For an offence triable by a district court, the procurator fiscal may offer the offender the option of paying a fine (a fiscal fine). Refusal will result in prosecution.

* For certain minor road-traffic offences, a police officer or traffic warden may issue a fixed-penalty notice. Failure to pay will result in the penalty being recovered as a fine.

* In the case of other minor road-traffic offences, the procurator fiscal may offer the alternative of paying a fixed penalty. If such an offer is accepted, and payment made, no prosecution is brought. In the case of an endorsable offence, the relevant penalty points are also added to the offender's driving licence.

Even where there appears to be sufficient evidence to prosecute, the procurator fiscal is entitled to decide not to prosecute if the offence is trivial or it is otherwise not in the public interest.

8.3 The system of public prosecution: the Crown Office and procurators fiscal

The Lord Advocate is the ministerial head of the Crown Office and the procurator fiscal service, and head of the systems of criminal prosecution and the investigation of deaths. His appointment is political and may change with a change of the Scottish Executive. While the Lord Advocate is accountable to the Scottish Parliament for the operation of the department in his charge, he is not required to justify any particular exercise of his discretion as prosecutor, either to the courts or to the Scottish Parliament. The independence of the Lord Advocate in his capacity as the head of the systems of criminal prosecution and the investigation of deaths in Scotland is preserved by the Scotland Act 1998.

The Crown Office and the procurator fiscal service is responsible for the preparation of prosecutions in the High Court, the sheriff court and the district court in Scotland. The Crown Office is responsible for the legal and administrative direction of the procurator fiscal service. Ultimate responsibility for criminal prosecution and the investigation of deaths rests with the Lord Advocate.

A few public authorities have statutory powers to prosecute for specific offences (for example, the Health and Safety Executive and HM Customs and Excise, and local authorities over non-attendance at school). In practice, these authorities usually prosecute through the procurator fiscal.

The system in Scotland is one of public prosecution. Private prosecution, where the victim undertakes a prosecution rather than the Crown, although rare is possible but requires the agreement of the Lord Advocate.

8.4 Summary and solemn procedure

In criminal cases, the main distinction is between summary and solemn procedure. The decision about which procedure to use is taken by the procurator fiscal or Crown counsel, and depends on the seriousness of the crime, and the previous convictions of the accused person, if any. More serious cases are prosecuted under solemn procedure, on 'indictment', either before a sheriff and jury or a High Court judge and jury. Some very serious crimes, such as murder, attempted murder, rape, attempted rape, and culpable homicide must be prosecuted under solemn procedure and may only be prosecuted in the High Court.

Summary cases are tried before a sheriff without a jury in the sheriff court, or before a magistrate or justices of the peace in the district court. Solemn procedure trials take place before a sheriff and jury in the sheriff court, or a judge and jury in the High Court. As with civil cases, criminal cases involve each side presenting its evidence to a judge, and a jury if there is one. A fundamental principal of criminal law is that the accused person is presumed innocent and the onus of proof is with the prosecution. The standard of proof is 'proof beyond reasonable doubt', which is a higher test than the 'balance of probabilities' test required in civil cases.

8.4.1 Bail

Under summary and solemn procedure an accused person is entitled to be released on bail. The sheriff or judge has a duty to consider whether to grant or refuse bail on the first appearance in court, with or without the need for an application to be made by the accused. It is at the discretion of the courts to grant bail. In determining whether it is appropriate for bail to be granted, the courts will take account of public safety and securing justice, and take into account any previous convictions. An accused person and the prosecutor have a right of appeal to the High Court against a decision of a sheriff in relation to bail at various stages in the proceedings.

If someone is released on bail this is subject to a set of conditions designed to ensure that the accused will be available for enquiry, will appear in court when required, will not commit an offence while on bail and will not interfere with witnesses or obstruct justice. A deposit of money is not usually required, but is possible in special circumstances.

8.5 Summary procedure

In most summary cases, the police will not arrest the person charged with the crime, especially if he or she appears to be normally law-abiding and has somewhere to stay. The accused person will be cited, that is summoned, to appear at the sheriff court or district court at a particular day and time.

8.5.1 Pre-trial procedure

The accused person receives a 'complaint', setting out where and when he or she must attend court, the accused person's name and address and a description of the alleged offence or offences he or she is accused of. Where the offence has been created by statute, there will be a notice of penalties that will apply to the accused person if convicted.

8.5.2 First hearing

Usually someone accused of a crime must appear personally to plead guilty or not guilty. Someone pleading guilty may be sentenced there and then, and if the judge is considering a prison sentence the accused person **must** be present. If an accused person pleads not guilty a trial date will be fixed, when the prosecution will have to prove their case.

It is possible for an accused person to plead guilty by letter and so have the case dealt with more quickly.

8.5.3 Intermediate diet

Between the first hearing and the trial, an additional hearing, the 'intermediate diet', is held. The accused person must attend, and is asked whether he or she still continues to plead not guilty, and the judge can ask both sides whether they are prepared for trial. Where the accused person is in custody, a trial must begin within 40 days of the commencement of the period of custody. If this does not happen, the accused person is freed and is immune from further prosecution for the offence.

If, at the intermediate diet, the accused person changes his or her plea to guilty, the judge may sentence him or her there and then, but would normally defer sentence to a later diet after consideration of social background reports about the accused person.

8.5.4 Trial

At the trial, the accused person may be represented by a solicitor, an advocate or a solicitor-advocate, or may represent himself or herself. The accused person will be asked again whether he or she is pleading not guilty, or may plead guilty to a modified charge. If pleading guilty, sentence will be passed once the judge hears any 'pleas in mitigation' and considers the accused person's previous convictions, if any. If the accused person continues to plead not guilty, evidence is led, first by the procurator fiscal, for the prosecution, then by the defence. Most of the evidence involves statements by witnesses who can be cross-examined by the opposing sides.

The judge has to decide whether he or she considers that the prosecution has proved the case beyond all reasonable doubt. Normally the decision is pronounced at once. If it is 'not guilty' or 'not proven' the accused person is discharged. The effect in both cases is the same – the accused person is immune from further criminal court action in relation to the offence. If the accused person is found guilty, then any previous convictions and pleas in mitigation are considered before sentence is passed. Summary cases cannot be sent to the High Court for sentence.

8.6   Solemn procedure

In more serious cases, the procurator fiscal may decide that the offence should be prosecuted 'on indictment', that is, under solemn procedure. In these cases, he or she presents a 'petition' to a sheriff which names the accused person, states the charge and seeks warrant to arrest the accused, search his or her premises, cite witnesses and examine the accused.

8.6.1 Pre-trial procedure

Once the accused person has had an opportunity of consulting a solicitor, he or she will go before a sheriff for judicial examination. This takes place in private with only the sheriff clerk, procurator fiscal, the accused person's solicitor and police escorts present. At this stage the procurator fiscal can ask the accused person a few questions about his or her response to the charge and any confession alleged to have been made. The procurator fiscal is also allowed to ask questions that might obtain admissions about the offence from the accused. A record of the examination may be used in evidence at a subsequent trial.

After the judicial examination, the procurator fiscal prepares the case by taking statements from witnesses and making other enquiries. Crown counsel then have to decide what the charge should be, and whether the case should go ahead under summary or solemn procedure, or whether to drop the case.

If the case is to proceed, the accused is served with an indictment, setting out the offences charged and a list of the evidence to be led at the trial, such as medical reports, and the names of Crown witnesses. The accused person is cited in the indictment to appear at a trial.

There are strict rules in Scots law that prevent an accused person spending an unduly long period in custody before trial. Where an accused person is in custody, he or she cannot be detained for more than 80 days without an indictment being served, and the trial must begin within 110 days, or the accused person must be freed. Where an accused person is on bail, (see 8.4.1), the trial must begin within twelve months of the first appearance, otherwise the trial cannot proceed. In all of these circumstances the accused person then becomes immune from further prosecution of the crime charged.

In solemn procedure in the sheriff court, a 'first diet' is held to find out whether the case is ready to go to trial. At this first diet, the court can also deal with any objections raised by the accused person, or consider any special defence. Objections that can be raised at this stage include, for example, that the crime in the indictment does not amount to a crime in terms of the law of Scotland, and special defences include alibi, self-defence, incrimination (that is, that someone else committed the crime), and insanity. There are similar rules for solemn proceedings in the High Court.

8.6.2 Trial

Criminal juries are always made up of 15 members of the public. Each side is allowed to object to individual jurors if they have a good reason, for instance, that they have known bad feeling towards the accused. The trial then proceeds in a similar way to a summary case, the main difference being that the prosecution has to convince the jury, not the judge, of the guilt of the accused person beyond reasonable doubt.

After all the evidence has been presented, by the prosecution and the defence, both sides address the jury. The judge then advises the jury on the relevant law and the issues for them to consider in reaching their decision. The judge can instruct them to return a verdict of not guilty in relation to any particular offence if not enough evidence of that offence has been presented.

The jury can give its verdict immediately, but more usually retires to consider it. The jury can decide a verdict by a majority, and the verdict can be guilty, not proven or not guilty. To reach a verdict of guilty, at least eight jurors have to vote for this. Where the verdict is guilty, the Crown will normally ask the judge to pass sentence. At that stage the Crown advises the judge of any previous convictions that it wishes the judge to take into account in deciding the sentence.

The defence can make a plea in mitigation on behalf of the accused person. The judge then passes sentence, either immediately or after consideration of social background reports about the accused person. A sheriff can refer the case to the High Court for sentence if it is felt that any sentence he or she can pass is inadequate.

8.7   Penalties

Any person convicted of a criminal offence may receive the following penalties:

* fine;

* admonition (a warning);

* period of imprisonment or detention in a young offenders' institution;

* community-service order (available in some courts only);

* probation;

* a compensation order which requires the convicted person to pay compensation to the victim, and can be combined with another penalty.

Failure to pay a fine can result in imprisonment, or 'supervised attendance orders' may be imposed. A supervised attendance order is an order requiring an offender to do work or attend instructional sessions for from ten to one hundred hours, supervised by the social work department. The court can also make an absolute discharge, which means no penalty is imposed and no conviction is recorded against the accused.

The maximum amount of a fine or period of imprisonment is limited in summary procedure. In solemn procedure, the only limits are those which are defined in statute for crimes created by statute.

8.8   Appeals

Someone convicted of a criminal offence in a summary case can appeal against conviction or sentence or both. Someone who has pled guilty can still appeal against the sentence imposed. The judge who made the original decision 'states a case' to the High Court, sitting as the Court of Criminal Appeal. The stated case contains a list of the charges, and the judge sets out the facts that were proved or admitted, and gives reasons for his or her decision. A convicted person can also appeal if there was something wrong with the procedure at the trial.

The Crown can also appeal, on a point of law only, against the judge's decision, or because of a procedural irregularity.

The High Court can either send the case back to the original court with directions, agree with the original verdict, set aside the verdict and either quash the conviction or substitute an amended verdict of guilty, or call for a new prosecution.

In solemn procedure, there are similar rules for appeals. However, the Lord Advocate has the right to refer a case resulting in an acquittal to the High Court for a decision on a point of law (although this does not affect the acquittal), and the Crown has a right of appeal against sentence on the grounds of undue leniency.

Since the Criminal Justice (Scotland) Act 1995, the right of appeal has been subject to the granting of leave to appeal by the High Court. A single High Court judge considers applications for leave to appeal and only if leave is granted would any appeal proceed to a hearing.

Like the Court of Session, the High Court has an equitable power, its *nobile officium*, which it may use to deal with unusual or unforeseen circumstances, or where there is no common law or statutory remedy and no other form of review appears possible or appropriate, or to avoid deadlock, injustice or oppression. It is not an alternative to other forms of appeal.

8.9 The Scottish Criminal Cases Review Commission

The Scottish Criminal Cases Review Commission is a statutory body set up by the Criminal Procedure (Scotland) Act 1995 to review alleged miscarriages of justice in Scotland. If the Commission believes that a miscarriage of justice may have occurred in a criminal conviction in a Scottish court, it can refer the case to the Court of Criminal Appeal for review. It will then be heard in the same way as any other appeal.

Where a jury has found a person guilty, he or she may at any time make an application to the Commission if he or she thinks something is wrong with the conviction. However, since the point of an application is to get a case referred to the Court of Criminal Appeal, in practice the Commission will not consider a petition while an appeal is pending or while an appeal could still be lodged.

8.10 Further reading

Gane, C H W & Stoddart, C N, *Casebook on Scottish Criminal Law*, 3rd edition. W Green, Edinburgh, 2000. £40.

Harper, J Ross, *A Fingertip Guide to Criminal Law*, 4th edition. Butterworth, Edinburgh, 1999. £42.

Crown Office and Procurator Fiscal Public Website: http://www.crownoffice.gov.uk

9

The personnel of the law

9.1   Judges

The judiciary in Scotland has two distinctive characteristics. First, in civil and criminal litigation, far greater use is made of full-time legally qualified judges than elsewhere in the United Kingdom, where lay magistrates play a greater role in family law and summary criminal cases. Nevertheless, many prosecutions in Scotland for minor offences are dealt with in lay summary courts. Second, in contrast to the general practice elsewhere in Europe, professional judges are drawn from legal practitioners, rather than persons specially trained to be judges throughout their careers.

9.1.1 Judges in the superior courts

The judges of the Court of Session are the senior permanent judges and technically they are Senators of the College of Justice. Appointments to the Court of Session are made by the Sovereign, although in practice the Lord President of the Court of Session and the Lord Justice-Clerk are nominated by the Prime Minister on the recommendation of the First Minister. The Prime Minister can only put forward candidates nominated by the First Minister. The Prime Minister also makes recommendations for the appointment of the two Scottish judges in the House of Lords.

Those eligible to be appointed as Senators are sheriffs and sheriffs principal of five years' standing and advocates (see 9.3.1) and solicitors (see 9.3.2) with five years' right of audience in the Court of Session. They are appointed by the Sovereign on the recommendation of the First Minister, following consultation with the Lord President. On appointment, they take the courtesy title of 'Lord' followed by their surname or a territorial title (Lord Rodger, Lord Sutherland). They are not members of the House of Lords, although some have been made life peers.

Senators appointed prior to 31 March 1995 must retire at the age of 75. Those appointed after that date must retire at the age of 70, but they are eligible to continue to sit as retired judges until they are 75. They can be removed from office (see 14.4.2).

Temporary judges may be appointed by the First Minister from among retired judges and those eligible to be appointed as Senators.

The Lord President of the Court of Session, Scotland's most senior judge, is also the Lord Justice-General of the High Court of Justiciary, and all Court of Session judges are also High Court judges. Temporary judges of the Court of Session are also temporary judges of the High Court.

The Scottish Executive is expected to set up an independent Judicial Appointments Board to handle the appointment of judges.

9.1.2 Sheriffs

Sheriffs, including sheriffs principal, are appointed by the Sovereign on the recommendation of the First Minster, who must first consult the Lord President of the Court of Session. Those eligible for appointment as sheriffs are advocates and solicitors of at least ten years' standing. Sheriffs principal are usually appointed from Queen's Counsel and those who are sheriffs already. Sheriffs appointed prior to 31 March 1995 must retire at the age of 72. Those appointed after that date must retire at the age of 70. They can be removed from office (see 14.4.3).

Floating sheriffs are permanent full-time sheriffs appointed to sit wherever required throughout Scotland's 49 sheriff courts. They can be removed from office (see 14.4.3).

Part-time sheriffs are appointed by Scottish Ministers to sit as and where necessary to assist with the pressure of business. There is provision for up to 60 part-time sheriffs at any one time. They are usually practising solicitors or advocates and may be appointed for up to five years. They do not sit in a court where they would normally appear as a practitioner. They can be removed from office (see 14.4.3).

The Scottish Executive is expected to set up an independent Judicial Appointments Board that would identify a 'slate' of appropriate candidates from whom the First Minister could make appropriate recommendations.

9.1.3 Justices of the peace in the district courts

District courts are presided over by lay justices of the peace, except in Glasgow where there are also salaried stipendiary magistrates. Stipendiary magistrates are appointed by the local authority from solicitors or advocates of at least five years' standing. 'Full justices' are appointed by the First Minister in the name of the Sovereign and on the recommendation of local justices of the peace advisory committees. They can be removed from office (see 14.4.4).

Local authorities may also nominate their members to serve as 'signing justices'. They do not sit in court but are available for signing warrants, etc.

At the age of 70, all justices are put on the 'supplemental list' and are available only for signing duties.

9.2 The public prosecutors

The Lord Advocate is the principal law officer of the Crown in Scotland. He is assisted by the Solicitor General for Scotland and a number of advocates depute who are the public prosecutors in the High Court. Advocates depute are appointed by the Lord Advocate from practising advocates and are known collectively as 'Crown counsel'. They devote almost all their practice to Crown work and during the period of their appointment do not engage in any criminal defence work. Crown counsel work along with a small permanent staff of civil servants, headed by the Crown Agent, in the Crown Office in Edinburgh.

The procurators fiscal are the public prosecutors in the sheriff and district courts. They are full-time civil servants, independent of the judiciary. They must be advocates or solicitors, and are usually solicitors. The police report details of a crime to the procurator fiscal, who has absolute discretion whether to prosecute, subject to the general direction and control of the Crown Office.

9.3 The legal profession: advocates and solicitors

The legal profession in Scotland has two branches: advocates (who correspond to barristers elsewhere in the United Kingdom) and solicitors. A person can move from one branch to another but cannot simultaneously be a member of both. There are about 680 advocates and 8,500 solicitors in Scotland.

9.3.1 Advocates

Members of the Faculty of Advocates are those who have been admitted to practise before the Court of Session. They can also present cases in the other superior courts in Scotland, the House of Lords, the Judicial Committee of the Privy Council, the European Court of Justice, the European Court of Human Rights and a wide range of tribunals, enquiries and other such proceedings. They can also appear before all the lower courts in Scotland. The Dean, who is its elected leader with responsibility for professional conduct and discipline, heads the Faculty of Advocates.

Approximately 417 members of the Faculty of Advocates are practising advocates. The remaining members include judges, sheriffs, academics and retired members.

For appearances in court, advocates are briefed by solicitors. The public cannot instruct advocates directly. Advocates also give their opinions on difficult or important legal problems referred to them by solicitors and, exceptionally, by others, and may supplement their practice by appearing before certain administrative tribunals and inquiries. Each advocate practises on his or her own; partnerships are not permitted. Practising advocates are either seniors or juniors. They enter as a junior and after ten to fifteen years' practice may apply through the Lord Justice-General to be appointed Queen's Counsel by the Queen. This is known as 'taking silk' from the silk gowns worn by QCs in court. As a QC or senior, an advocate is entitled to be accompanied by a junior to assist him or her in the conduct of a case but may choose not to do so.

The Faculty of Advocates has its own professional examinations. However, prospective advocates usually obtain exemption from these by obtaining an appropriate law degree from a Scottish university and a Diploma in Legal Practice. Prospective advocates must undergo a period of training in a solicitor's office, followed by training under a practising advocate (known as 'devilling' and the trainee advocate a 'devil'). During this period he or she must take Faculty of Advocates' examinations in certain practical subjects for which a law degree gives no exemption.

9.3.2 Solicitors

All practising solicitors must be members of the Law Society of Scotland, the statutory governing body of Scottish solicitors. Among other things, the Law Society regulates admission to the solicitors' profession, represents solicitors in their relations with government, other bodies and the public; makes representations for law reform; enforces standards of professional conduct; and maintains a guarantee fund from which payments are made to people who have suffered pecuniary loss because of the dishonesty of a solicitor in practice (see 14.2.1).

Solicitors undertake most of the litigation in the sheriff courts. Most civil work concerns divorce and related family matters and actions for the recovery of debts. Criminal work covers a wide variety of cases. Many solicitors in private practice engage in the buying and selling of property, estate management and management of trusts and executries. Many are licensed to advise on financial investments.

The majority of solicitors are in private practice, that is, they practise alone or as partners in firms of solicitors. However, many are employed as assistants to solicitors in private practice and a considerable minority are employed by local authorities, central government departments (including procurators fiscal and officials of the Crown Office), by industrial and commercial companies, and by public authorities and bodies.

Like the Faculty of Advocates, the Law Society has its own professional examinations, from which solicitors may obtain exemption by including the necessary professional subjects in a law degree from a Scottish university. A solicitor wishing to practice on his or her own or in partnership must take out an annual practising certificate from the Law Society which keeps the Roll of Solicitors.

9.3.3 Solicitor-advocates

While solicitors cannot appear before the superior courts, they can seek 'extended rights of audience', which allow them to represent clients as solicitor-advocates in the Court of Session, the High Court of Justiciary, the House of Lords and before the Judicial Committee of the Privy Council. Solicitors with at least five years' continuous experience of court work may apply to practise in the superior civil or criminal courts or both. They must undergo an induction course, observe cases in court, attend a training course in the work of courts, and pass examinations on subjects related to practice in the superior courts. There are certain exemptions for solicitors with appropriate experience.

9.4 Sheriff clerks and clerks to the district court

The sheriff clerk is a court official who is responsible for the administration of cases. He or she calls the cases in court, and sits in court during civil hearings and criminal trials and notes the outcome. Sheriff clerks are civil servants who are employed by the Scottish Court Service and are responsible for the day-to-day running of the sheriff court under the supervision of the sheriffs and the sheriff principal.

Clerks to the district court are members of the legal staff of the local authority. They are legally qualified and are responsible for the organisation of the court and the provision of legal advice to the bench.

9.5 Witnesses

A person who is cited as a witness at a criminal trial must attend court at the time and date specified. A witness who does not attend and has not been excused can be arrested and prosecuted. He or she has a duty to cooperate with 'both sides', that is, to give a statement to the procurator fiscal and the defence.

Witnesses do not get paid, but in criminal cases can claim expenses and loss of earnings. In civil cases it is up to each side to arrange for their witnesses to be in court.

In court, a witness may take the oath or affirm. Witnesses are examined first by the side that called them, to bring out the story in the witness's own words. Cross-examination by the other side is designed to challenge aspects of the witness's story. Re-examination may take place to try to dispel any doubts raised. A witness who is found to have been untruthful risks prosecution for perjury.

9.6 Jurors

Jurors are involved in all criminal trials under solemn procedure, where the jury is fifteen. They may also be involved in some civil actions in the Court of Session, where the jury is twelve.

Potential jurors are selected at random from the electoral register. They must be between the ages of 18 and 65, ordinarily resident in the United Kingdom for at least five years, and registered as an elector. Certain individuals connected with the legal profession are ineligible; people suffering from a mental illness are disqualified; and certain ex-offenders are ineligible. Some people may be excused jury duty, for example, doctors, nurses, dentists, MPs, members of the armed services, the clergy, people who have served on a jury in the last five years, and certain people with disabilities or medical conditions.

Jurors are chosen by lot from a larger number of potential jurors summoned for the purpose. The first fifteen in a criminal trial, or twelve in a civil action, form a jury. Both the prosecution and the defence can object to up to three jurors without reason and others with good reason. Jurors may sit on a number of juries over the period of a week, or on one jury for longer.

Jurors must consider the evidence presented by each side and, subject to directions in matters of law by the presiding judge or sheriff, to reach a verdict on one or more matters of fact or of mixed fact and law. In a criminal case, at least eight jurors must be satisfied 'beyond reasonable doubt' that the accused committed the crime charged. In a civil case, at least seven jurors must be satisfied 'on the balance of probabilities' that, for example, the accident to the pursuer was caused by the fault of the defender and, if so, at what sum damages should be assessed.

The jurors choose a spokesperson from among themselves and he or she announces the verdict orally when asked to do so by the clerk of court.

9.7 Messengers-at-arms and sheriff officers

The courts and their officials do not carry out the functions of collecting sums due under decrees of the Scottish courts, and of enforcing debts due under court decrees in the event of the debtor's failure to pay. After granting a decree, the pursuer is left to recover the debt from the other person, and if unsuccessful must instruct a messenger-at-arms or sheriff officer to enforce the decree.

Messengers-at-arms enforce Court of Session decrees and sheriff officers enforce sheriff-court decrees. In practice, however, many sheriff officers are also messengers-at-arms.

Messengers-at-arms are appointed and disciplined by the Lord Lyon King of Arms. Sheriff officers are appointed and disciplined by the appropriate sheriff principal. Messengers and sheriff officers charge fees that are prescribed by rules made by the Court of Session. Like solicitors, they may be in business on their own or in partnerships.

10

The administration of the
Scottish legal system

10.1 Introduction

The administration of the Scottish legal system has two main aspects: first, the organisation and administration of the courts and ancillary services; and second, the oversight and review of the law by Scottish Ministers and the promotion of law reform.

10.2 The organisation and administration of the courts

The administration of the supreme courts is the responsibility of the Lord President and the Lord Justice-General. In the case of the sheriff courts, this function is carried out partly by the sheriffs principal and partly by the First Minister.

The supreme courts, the Court of Session and the High Court of Justiciary, enact the rules governing their own procedures and those of the sheriff and lay summary courts. The statutory Rules Council and the Sheriff Court Rules Council, consisting of judges and legal practitioners (and in the case of the Sheriff Court Rules Council, two lay people), advise the supreme courts on amendments to the rules.

The First Minister is responsible for the central organisation and administration of the sheriff courts and, to a lesser extent, the supreme courts. He or she also decides on the number of sheriffs in each sheriffdom, and he or she may alter the boundaries of sheriffdoms and districts, create new ones and fix the places where the sheriff court is to be held. This responsibility is discharged by one of his or her ministers. The sheriff principal is responsible for the speedy and efficient conduct of business in his or her sheriffdom.

Some sheriff courts have their own users' advisory committees who consider administrative matters to do with processing the business of that court. These tend to concentrate on criminal business.

The Scottish Court Service is an executive agency, which is responsible for such non-legal, practical matters as the proper accommodation and staffing of the courts, the pay and conditions of service of clerks of court and other officers who assist the judges in the running of the courts. It is part of the Scottish Executive Justice Department, the government department responsible for reporting to the First Minister on the performance of the Scottish Court Service.

The Courts Group, which is also part of the Scottish Executive Justice Department, is responsible, on behalf of the Lord Advocate, for the general oversight of certain parts of the legal system that are connected with the Scottish courts. These include, for example, the jurisdiction and procedure of the courts in civil proceedings, the rules for enforcement of court orders in civil proceedings, and policy functions such as reviewing the law of evidence, and civil jurisdiction in the courts.

The local authorities, advised by justices' committees, administer the district courts, providing them, for example, with buildings and clerks of court. The justices' committees approve the duty rota of justices and administer training schemes for justices set up by the First Minister.

10.3 Ministerial supervision of the legal system

The First Minister has overall responsibility for the Scottish legal system, although this is largely exercised by the Minister for Justice. His or her responsibilities include specific duties, for example, in relation to the appointment of judges. However, judges, whether lay or professional, are not in any way subject to ministerial control and the independence of the courts is scrupulously observed.

Some of the functions of ministers are carried out by executive agencies, for example, the Scottish Court Service, and the Registers of Scotland Executive Agency.

General responsibility is shared with the two law officers. The junior law officer is the Solicitor General for Scotland. He or she is a legal adviser to and member of the Scottish Executive, and may appear for the executive in criminal or civil proceedings. Despite the title, the Solicitor General has always been an advocate. The senior law officer is the Lord Advocate. He or she is a member of the Scottish Executive, and is its chief legal adviser.

The Lord Advocate's department is responsible for drafting Scottish legislation. The Lord Advocate is responsible for prosecuting crime generally, through the Crown Office and the Crown Agent. In solemn criminal proceedings he or she is the named prosecutor (referred to as 'HM Advocate') and may appear himself or herself. In civil cases, the Lord Advocate sues on behalf of the executive and defends cases against it (referred to as 'Lord Advocate').

The Scotland Act 1998 created the post of Advocate General for Scotland, who is a minister of the United Kingdom government.

10.4   Agencies of law reform

The most important agency of law reform in Scotland is the Scottish Law Commission. The Commission is a permanent statutory body of five members who have a duty to keep the whole of the law of Scotland under review with a view to its systematic development and reform. It has responsibility for all areas of Scots law, including those reserved to the legislative competence of the United Kingdom Parliament. The Commission is supported by a permanent staff. The Lord Advocate appoints the part-time chairman, who is a judge seconded from the Court of Session, and three full-time and one part-time commissioners. They represent the judiciary, both branches of the legal profession and academic lawyers.

Law reform can be initiated by the Commission itself or jointly with the Law Commission in England and Wales. Proposals can also come from organisations or individuals. Scottish Ministers may also ask the Commission to undertake work on certain areas of the law. The Commission's work is approved by Scottish Ministers or on the basis of a reference from Scottish Ministers. Proposals for law reform are made in the form of published reports, often with draft legislation attached, which are submitted to Scottish Ministers. In matters reserved to the United Kingdom Parliament, the report will also be submitted to the Secretary of State for Scotland.

Occasionally, Royal Commissions and departmental committees or working parties are set up by ministers as temporary part-time bodies to make proposals for reform in particular areas of the law.

The Scottish Executive and United Kingdom government departments may themselves publish tentative proposals or firm proposals for law reform in order to consult interested bodies before the introduction of legislation. The Scottish Executive refers to tentative proposals as 'consultation documents' and firm proposals as 'consultations on draft legislation'. United Kingdom government departments refer to them as 'green papers' and 'white papers' respectively.

10.5 Other public offices

Apart from the departments of the Scottish Executive and the United Kingdom government directly under ministerial control, a number of small autonomous public offices or departments, staffed by civil servants, provide essential services for the legal system. Some have been referred to elsewhere (see 4.5 and 8.3).

The Registers of Scotland Executive Agency maintains a number of public registers including the General Register of Sasines, which is a register of title deeds relating to land transactions in Scotland. Under the Land Registration (Scotland) Act 1979, the Land Register of Scotland was established, which will eventually record all interests in land, and will in time completely replace the General Register of Sasines.

The General Register Office for Scotland is a department of the Scottish Executive responsible for the registration of births, deaths, marriages, divorces and adoptions in Scotland, and for carrying out periodic censuses of Scotland's population. Other registries include the Register of Friendly Societies in Scotland, and the register of companies incorporated in Scotland under the Companies Act maintained by Companies House.

10.6 Further reading

Crown Office and Procurator Fiscal Public Website:
http://www.crownoffice.gov.uk

Scottish Executive Justice Department:
http://www.scotland.gov.uk/who/dept_justice.asp

An Introduction to the Scottish Court Service. Available free from the Scottish Court Service, Hayweight House, 23 Lauriston Street, Edinburgh EH3 9DQ.

See also: http://www.scotcourts.gov.uk

11

Judicial review

Judicial review of administrative action is a means of challenging in the courts the way in which decisions are reached by public authorities. Its purpose is to ensure that they act within the law. It is distinct from appeal, which challenges the merits of a decision.

All public authorities – government departments, local authorities, statutory corporations, administrative tribunals, and the like – exist to perform functions defined and limited in varying degrees of detail by legislation or the rules of common law.

A public authority acts outwith the law (*ultra vires*) if it assumes a power that it does not by law possess, or if it uses its powers to defeat the objects for which the powers were conferred on it or for purposes that differ from those prescribed by law, or it fails to exercise its powers in accordance with the procedure laid down by law. Any person whose rights are injured, or threatened with injury, by an *ultra vires* or negligent act of a public authority, or by any failure of the authority to perform its statutory duties, may bring an action of judicial review to obtain the appropriate remedy.

Legal proceedings for judicial review can be raised only in the Court of Session. If the Court decides that the action or decision complained of is illegal, it can provide a number of different remedies, the more important of which are:

* Declarator: an order declaring the existence of a legal right.

* Interdict: an order that stops the public authority from doing something that is illegal. Interdict cannot be made against the Crown. The Court may grant interim interdict to maintain the *status quo* pending the Court's final decision.

* Reduction: an order that invalidates the decision complained of.

* Damages: an order awarding compensation for any damage caused by the negligent exercise of statutory powers or duties.

The characteristic flexibility of Scottish civil procedure enables all or any of these remedies to be obtained in one action.

The enactment of the Scotland Act 1998 and the Human Rights Act 1998 created new opportunities for judicial review. The availability of human rights directly enforceable before United Kingdom courts and the creation of the Scottish Parliament are likely to lead to the growth of judicial review and also to confirm its importance in the United Kingdom's constitution.

The Scotland Act provides for the United Kingdom or Scottish Law Officers to refer a bill of the Scottish Parliament to the Judicial Committee of the Privy Council to settle a question of *vires*. A bill may not be submitted for Royal Assent if it is the subject of a reference to the Judicial Committee. The Scotland Act also provides for dealing with the consequences of Acts of the Scottish Parliament or actions of the Scottish Executive that are found to be outwith their powers.

For example, a Scottish Bill is outwith the competence of the parliament if it conflicts with the European Convention on Human Rights as incorporated in the Human Rights Act, and the Scotland Act prevents a member of the Scottish Executive from making legislation if it is incompatible with the convention. The courts have powers to limit the retrospective effects of such Acts or actions. Provision is also made for the United Kingdom Parliament to make subordinate legislation to remedy the defect.

In certain activities of public authorities, for example, compulsory purchase of land, town and country planning, statutes provide for judicial review of whether the statutory procedures have been complied with.

12

Legal aid

12.1 Introduction

Legal aid is financial help from the state with legal costs. In Scotland, the Scottish Legal Aid Board administers legal aid.

Legal aid can be made available for civil and criminal actions and for general advice and assistance with legal problems. It is also available 'in respect of certain proceedings relating to children'.

There are strict financial limits on who qualifies for legal aid. Some people who qualify for legal aid have to make a financial contribution. Where a civil action for the recovery of money, property or expenses succeeds, the Scottish Legal Aid Board is entitled to be repaid first, subject to regulations that provide for certain exclusions to this rule. Someone who is legally aided would not pay the expenses of his or her own solicitor if he or she lost the case but may have to pay the legal expenses of the other side.

Proposals for the provision of information and legal advice and assistance through community legal services in Scotland are being developed. This would provide an integrated network of legal services throughout the community, which would help people involved in civil disputes.

12.2 Advice and Assistance

Advice and Assistance is available to people with limited income and assets to obtain advice from a solicitor or, where appropriate, from an advocate, on any matter of Scots law. This includes, for example, questions relating to marriage, debt, employment, personal injury, landlord and tenant, neighbours, consumer law, and wills. It does not usually cover representation in a court or tribunal, although a solicitor can help with the preparation of a case or the negotiation of a settlement of a claim in such proceedings. However, there are exceptions for certain criminal and civil proceedings, proceedings under Part V of the Mental Health (Scotland) Act 1984 and proceedings before certain tribunals.

12.3 Legal aid in civil proceedings

Legal aid may be available where a dispute or claim can only be settled by court action, or where someone is defending a civil case. For example, where someone has received Advice and Assistance on a legal matter and no resolution has been possible, he or she may be advised that the only course is to start a civil action. This type of legal aid covers proceedings in the sheriff court, the Court of Session, the House of Lords, the Lands Valuation Appeal Court, the Lands Tribunal for Scotland, the Scottish Land Court, the Restrictive Practices Court, the Employment Appeal Tribunal and the Judicial Committee of the Privy Council on appeal from the Court of Session.

All types of action are included except actions for defamation, verbal injury, election petitions, simplified actions of divorce, small claims proceedings at first instance and certain proceedings at first instance under the Debtors (Scotland) Act 1987. Legal aid may also be available for mediation in some cases.

To be legally aided, an applicant must be financially eligible and the following conditions apply:

* legal aid is not available if someone else is prepared to assist or back the applicant, such as a trade union or insurance company;

* there must be sound grounds for taking, defending or being party to the proceedings;

* legal aid is not available if it is unreasonable in the circumstances to grant it − for instance, it would be unreasonable to grant legal aid to take a minor action in a superior court if a less expensive action in the sheriff court would be sufficient.

Where legal aid is refused, the decision can be reviewed.

12.4 Legal aid in criminal proceedings

Criminal Legal Aid is available to the accused person in prosecutions brought in the district court, the sheriff court, the High Court and in appeals from all criminal courts.

In solemn proceedings, the court decides whether to grant legal aid. It is also for the court to decide whether to grant legal aid where a person who has not previously been sentenced to imprisonment or detention has been convicted in summary proceedings and the court is considering such a sentence. In summary cases, legal aid may be available either by application to the Board or by Assistance By Way of Representation (see 12.4.3).

12.4.1 Accused person in custody

An accused person who is taken into custody, even if released on bail, will usually have a right to automatic free legal aid from the duty solicitor up to and including the first court appearance. A duty solicitor is available at every district and sheriff court to advise accused persons in custody. The duty solicitor can also represent someone appearing in an identification parade.

In summary cases, only the duty solicitor can represent someone by way of legal aid in his or her first appearance in court; the accused can select another solicitor at his or her own expense. In solemn cases, the accused can select the duty solicitor or another solicitor of his or her choice.

Under a pilot scheme, people in Edinburgh who want Criminal Legal Aid for a case in the Edinburgh courts can choose between a private solicitor or a Public Defence Solicitor employed by the Scottish Legal Aid Board. The continuation of the scheme beyond September 2003 will be decided by the Scottish Parliament.

12.4.2 Accused person not in custody

Advice and Assistance may be available to someone served with a summary complaint, depending on his or her financial circumstances. Where an accused person intends to plead not guilty, application for Criminal Legal Aid can only be made after that plea to the court. If granted, it will not cover the first appearance in court for the plea of not guilty and the accused has either to attend court personally to plead, or arrange for a solicitor to make a written plea on his or her behalf using advice and assistance.

12.4.3 Assistance By Way of Representation

Assistance By Way of Representation (ABWOR) allows a solicitor, in certain circumstances, to represent a client who is not in custody and who intends to plead guilty or has changed his or her plea to guilty, provided no application for legal aid has been made.

12.4.4 Appeal against conviction or sentence

Someone convicted in a criminal court can get advice on a question of appeal, using Advice and Assistance or under any existing legal aid cover for the initial proceedings. In a case where leave to appeal is needed and this is granted, the financial test is applied if it is needed. In other cases, legal aid will be granted where the Board decides that it is in the interests of justice to make legal aid available to the applicant.

12.5 Further reading

Scottish Legal Aid Board, *Guide to legal aid in Scotland*. Available free from the Scottish Legal Aid Board, 44 Drumsheugh Gardens, Edinburgh EH3 7SW.

See also: http://www.slab.org.uk

Stoddart, Charles N & Neilsen, Hugh S, *The Law and Practice of Legal Aid in Scotland*, 4th edition. T & T Clark, Edinburgh, 1994. £45.

13

Other sources of assistance

13.1 Citizens advice bureaux

Citizens advice bureaux form a network that covers Scotland. Most are organised by full-time managers and staffed by trained unpaid volunteers. The government funds the central support organisation, Citizens Advice Scotland, which provides training and a comprehensive information system, and sets standards for local bureaux. The local authorities provide local funding.

Citizens advice bureaux provide basic advice and assistance on legal problems with the support of Citizens Advice Scotland. Where legal services are required, bureaux can refer people to local solicitors or to legal clinics provided by local solicitors, often utilising the Advice and Assistance scheme (see 12.2).

13.2 Money advice services

Money advice services are specialised agencies set up to assist with debt problems arising from credit, mortgages and loans, etc. They are provided by citizens advice bureaux, local authority consumer advice and trading standards departments and independent advice agencies. They act as intermediaries for people with multiple debt problems by negotiating repayments on their behalf, so reducing the incidence of debt enforcement and bankruptcy. Money Advice Scotland supports some of the agencies and provides training and a forum for the exchange of views.

13.3 Law centres

Law centres are non-profit making charitable bodies staffed by legally-qualified advisers and support staff. They provide legal services in deprived areas not otherwise provided by traditional legal services, and specialise in areas such as social security, housing, consumer issues and immigration. They also provide training for local organisations and raise awareness of the law and legal issues. There is a growing number of law centres in Scotland, but they remain more heavily concentrated in urban areas.

13.4 Qualified conveyancers and executry practitioners

The Law Reform (Miscellaneous Provisions) (Scotland) Act 1990 provides for non-solicitors to become qualified conveyancers and executry practitioners. Provided they meet the requirements for training and qualifications, they can offer conveyancing services and executry services to the public for a fee. The Scottish Conveyancing and Executry Services Board regulates them.

Financial institutions, such as banks, building societies and insurance companies are similarly able to offer executry services, but they are not permitted to do conveyancing.

13.5 Trades unions

Some of the larger trades unions provide legal services for their members. These may be provided either by their own staff or through firms of solicitors, and may include advice on any legal problem, and if there is a case to be pursued how it may be financed, for example, by the union.

13.6 Insurance companies

Some insurance companies offer their policy holders advice on personal legal problems and legal protection insurance which covers the costs of legal actions in, for example, consumer disputes, claims for death or injury, claims connected with their homes, and claims connected with a contract of employment.

13.7 Para-legal services

Some non-legally-qualified practitioners provide advice and negotiation services for personal injury claims and employment matters. They are not permitted to represent someone in court.

14

Protection of the public

14.1 Introduction

The legal profession is largely self-regulating. However, there are a number of protections for solicitors' clients and rather fewer for clients of advocates. Solicitors' and advocates' professional bodies have their own internal complaints and disciplinary procedures, overseen by the Scottish Legal Services Ombudsman (see 14.6).

14.2 Solicitors

Solicitors must be covered by insurance against claims for damages (see 14.2.2), and they must contribute to a Guarantee Fund to provide protection for the public against dishonest solicitors. The Law Society also has powers to deal with complaints of professional misconduct, and with claims of inadequate professional services or excessive fees.

14.2.1 Dishonesty

The Law Society of Scotland maintains a Guarantee Fund from which compensation may be paid to people who have suffered loss because of the dishonesty of solicitors. The fund is a last resort after other remedies have been pursued and have failed. Solicitors make an annual contribution to the fund, and may be required to make additional payments to meet exceptional demands.

14.2.2 Professional negligence

A solicitor who does not exercise a reasonable standard of care and skill may be sued for consequential loss by a client, and possibly by third parties, on the grounds of negligence. Negligence may include failure to register documents and failing to start a court action within the required time limit. The Law Society requires all its members to be covered by its master policy of professional indemnity.

14.2.3 Inadequate professional services and excessive fees

Inadequate services are those that fall short of negligence. The Law Society has powers, on receiving a complaint from a solicitor's client, to order a reduction or waiver of fees, a refund, a rectification of errors and omissions, and payment to the complainer of up to £1000 as compensation for inconvenience.

If the Council of the Law Society regards the fees charged by a solicitor to be grossly excessive, and this is established by the Auditor of Court, it has the power to order a refund and suspend the solicitor from practice until this is done.

14.2.4 Discipline

In more serious cases, the Law Society will prosecute the solicitor before the Scottish Solicitors Discipline Tribunal.

The Scottish Solicitors Discipline Tribunal is composed of ten to fourteen solicitors and eight lay members. Where a solicitor has been convicted of an offence involving dishonesty or has been sentenced to imprisonment for not less than two years, and the matter has been brought to the attention of the tribunal by the Law Society, the tribunal can act on that alone. The tribunal also considers appeals by solicitors against determinations of inadequate professional service by the Law Society. On any other disciplinary view expressed by the Law Society, it would be for the solicitor to take advice and to consider the prospects of judicial review.

The tribunal has the power to strike off, suspend from practice, censure and fine a solicitor up to £10,000, and to restrict a solicitor in relation to practice, for example, to practising as an assistant with a firm. The tribunal also has powers similar to those of the Law Society when considering complaints of inadequate professional service. Its decisions are published, unless to do so would harm persons other than the solicitor, their partners and their families.

14.3 Advocates

Advocates, like other lawyers, may be held liable for negligent advice unconnected with court proceedings. Apart from that, the law is currently uncertain. The House of Lords has ruled on two occasions that, on public interest grounds, it was inappropriate for lawyers engaged in litigation to be subject to negligence claims. Although a different view was taken in an English case in 2000, certain of the grounds relied on would not apply in Scotland, and their Lordships expressly confirmed that the position in Scotland was not under consideration in that appeal.

14.3.1 Discipline

Anyone can complain about the behaviour of an advocate to the Dean of the Faculty of Advocates. The Dean can deal with the complaint himself or herself, and can impose a fine of up to £5,000 or order a repayment of fees or both. He or she may set up a committee to investigate issues of disputed fact and report back to him or her for disposal. Alternatively, he or she may refer the case to the Faculty's Disciplinary Tribunal, which is chaired by a retired judge or sheriff principal and has a formal procedure. The tribunal can impose a fine of up to £10,000, and may order suspension or expulsion of the advocate concerned. Decisions of the tribunal may be subject to judicial review in the Court of Session (see Chapter 11). The Faculty's disciplinary procedures are currently under review, and it is anticipated that a complaints committee, which will include lay representation, will in future decide all cases not referred to the tribunal.

14.4 Judges

14.4.1 Introduction

Someone who is dissatisfied with the outcome of a case, and who thinks that the judge or sheriff was wrong, can only appeal against their decision to a higher court, if a right of appeal exists in the particular circumstances.

14.4.2 Superior court judges

The First Minister, on the recommendation of the Scottish Parliament, may remove a superior court judge from office 'by reason of inability, neglect of duty, or misbehaviour'. If such a decision is under consideration, an investigating tribunal must be formed which reports its findings to the Scottish Parliament.

14.4.3 Sheriffs

The First Minister can also remove a sheriff from office. If, after investigation by the Lord President and the Lord Justice-Clerk, a sheriff is reported as not fit for office 'by reason of inability, neglect of duty, or misbehaviour' the First Minister may make a statutory instrument (subject to annulment by the Scottish Parliament) removing him or her. This happens very rarely.

Part-time sheriffs can be removed from office only by order of a tribunal of three members appointed by the Lord President of the Court of Session.

14.4.4 Justices of the peace

A full justice in a district court may be removed from office or be restricted to having the functions of a signing justice (see 9.1.3) only by order of a tribunal of three members appointed by the Lord President of the Court of Session.

14.5 Courts administration staff

The Scottish Court Service has a procedure for considering complaints about any of its services. These include the services provided by any members of the Principal Clerk's staff (in the supreme courts) or the Regional Sheriff Clerk's staff (in the sheriff courts).

14.6 The Scottish Legal Services Ombudsman

The ombudsman is an independent lay investigator, appointed by Scottish Ministers. The ombudsman cannot be a lawyer. He or she investigates and reports on complaints made against legal services professional organisations about the way they have dealt with a complaint against a practitioner. The professional organisations are the Law Society of Scotland, the Faculty of Advocates and the Scottish Conveyancing and Executry Services Board.

Any person who has a complaint against a legal practitioner that has been investigated by one of the professional bodies or one that the professional body has declined to investigate may complain to the ombudsman. Complaints to the ombudsman about unsatisfactory handling of a complaint by a professional body must be made within six months of the body's decision.

The ombudsman cannot over-rule the decisions of the professional body. He or she can only recommend a particular form of redress or further investigation on a particular complaint, or make general recommendations on dealing with complaints to the professional body or, where necessary, to Scottish Ministers. He or she may also take a case to the Scottish Solicitors Discipline Tribunal.

14.7 Further reading

Law Society of Scotland/Scottish Consumer Council, *Getting the best from your solicitor*. Law Society of Scotland, Edinburgh, 1999. Available free from The Law Society of Scotland, 26 Drumsheugh Gardens, Edinburgh EH3 7YR.

Law Society of Scotland: http://www.lawscot.org.uk/

Scottish Legal Services Ombudsman, *Annual Report, 2000*. The Stationery Office, Edinburgh, 2001. The current report can be also be found at

http://www.scot-legal-ombud.org.uk

General reading

Paterson, A A & Bates, T St J N, *The Legal System of Scotland*, 4th edition. W Green, Edinburgh, 1999. £30.

Walker, D M, *The Scottish Legal System*, 7th edition. W Green, Edinburgh, 1997. £40.

Index